Start Your Own

GRANT-WRITING BUSINESS

Additional titles in *Entrepreneur's* **Startup Series**

Start Your Own

Entrepreneur
MAGAZINE'S

startup

Start Your Own

GRANT-WRITING BUSINESS

Your Step-by-Step Guide to Success

Entrepreneur Press and Preethi Burkholder

EP
Entrepreneur
Press

Jere L. Calmes, Publisher
Managing Editor: Marla Markman
Cover Design: Beth Hansen-Winter
Production and Composition: Eliot House Productions

This publication is designed to provide accurate and authoritative information in regard to the subject matter covered. It is sold with the understanding that the publisher is not engaged in rendering legal, accounting or other professional services. If legal advice or other expert assistance is required, the services of a competent professional person should be sought.

Library of Congress Cataloging-in-Publication Data

    Start your own grant-writing business / by Entrepreneur Press and Preethi Burkholder.
      p.   cm.
   ISBN-13: 978-1-59918-159-2 (alk. paper)
   ISBN-10: 1-59918-159-2 (alk. paper)
      1. Proposal writing for grants. 2. Proposal writing for grants—Vocational guidance.
   3. Grants-in-aid. 4. New business enterprises—Management. I. Burkholder, Preethi.
   HG177.S73 2008
   658.15'224—dc22   2007040582

Printed in the United States of America

13 12 11 10 09 08   10 9 8 7 6 5 4 3 2

Contents

Preface

As a student, grants enabled me to pay for education, travel overseas, help needy people in developing countries, and research indigenous healing rituals in remote parts of Asia. These were exciting opportunities that I could not have afforded without philanthropic support. I won my first grant award as a junior in college. The travel grant gave me the opportunity to spend a summer in Switzerland and participate in a classical music festival. It was the first time that I was paid to travel overseas and gain an education at the same time. During graduate school, I shifted my focus of grant seeking into research and humanitarian work overseas. Early on, I realized money was out there for hard-working folks who sought external financial support to pursue their ambitions in life. Knowing how to secure that money was key.

After graduate school, I transferred my knowledge, skill, and experiences in writing grant applications for my education to help individuals and organizations obtain funds to further their own agendas. For many years, I volunteered my grant-writing skills before they started to earn me an income.

Today, I make an income as a grant writer in several different ways. I write proposals on behalf of individuals and organizations; publish books, articles, and newsletters on how to win grants; travel to different parts of the country and present grant-writing workshops; and raise grant money for nonprofit organizations in Sri Lanka. Through successful grantsmanship, I have been able to secure money, goods, and services to help others achieve their goals. I also have met fascinating people across the globe as a result of winning grants for various projects.

My experiences as a grant writer are compiled in this book. In it, I discuss:

- Researching funders and knowing where to look
- The art of the grant proposal
- Tips for entrepreneurs wanting to start their own grant-writing business
- Insider rules and tips for successful grant seeking.

It has been my goal to introduce this book as a single resource to readers, so that they don't need to buy a second or third book to learn the art of running a grant-writing business. This is the only grant-writing book you will ever need.

It is widely believed that winning a grant is a mysterious thing, restricted to a select few outstanding individuals. I have spent many years demystifying this perception. If you are willing to work hard and have the determination to succeed, much of the mystery of grant seeking can be lifted.

If there is one thing that has tested me most as a grant writer during the past decade, it is my ability to continue to believe in myself amid continuous rejection. A stoic resilience to rejection was not a trait that I was born with. But, it is a trait I have been gently forced to nurture as a grant writer. No grant writer has immunity from rejection.

Believing in yourself is a critical part of grant seeking. When you believe in yourself and commit to the hard work required to make your dreams come true, your self-esteem and confidence are enhanced, which subconsciously translates into a winning grant proposal.

There are two people who always reminded me to aim high and believe in myself. My parents showed me that I can be all I want to be, *if* I were willing to work hard, make sound choices in life, and cultivate a spiritual foundation. This book is for my parents, for all their sacrifices, tears, and hard work in raising me and giving me the best education they could offer. Words cannot express the gratitude I have to my dear father in heaven and my loving mother. Thank you, Thatha and Amma.

—Preethi Burkholder

To my loving father in heaven, Thatha,
and my loving mother, Amma.

Thank you for teaching me to write and
giving me an excellent education.

Choosing Grant
Writing for a Career Path

Philanthropy has never been greater. In 2005, the

Bill and Melinda Gates Foundation gave away $1,356,250,292

for charitable work in the United States and abroad. As more

people are giving away money for various causes, the job of

the grant writer is to secure funds for individuals, nonprofits, businesses, and governments. The grant writer is the vital connecting link between a funder and grant seeker.

Strike While the Iron Is Hot

Skilled grant writers are one of the most in-demand professionals today. They work as independent contractors, full- or part-time development officers, and freelancers. Prompted by the increasing demand to find new sources of funding, nonprofit agencies are always looking for help to identify these sources and take on grant-writing projects. Virtually every nonprofit needs a skilled grant writer, and there are hundreds of thousands of nonprofits currently in operation in the United States alone. Internationally, there are many more. This is a great time to start your own grant-writing business or to become a freelance grant writer.

The majority of grants are given to organizations that have a tax-exempt or nonprofit status. Also known as 501(c)(3) status, these organizations operate as charities and usually offer promise of helping their communities at the local, national, and sometimes international levels. While some of the larger organizations have a grant writer on staff, this isn't the case for the majority of nonprofits currently in operation. Indeed, the career of a grant writer is still in an infant stage, and only a handful of individuals are skilled at the profession.

If you are considering a career change, grant writing may be for you. An unhappy job situation can influence every other aspect of your life: your mental health, your relationships, and your social life. Being unhappy with your job may also stunt your potential if you are crippled by a work environment where you are made to feel inadequate. Instead, you may consider becoming a skilled grant writer and starting your own grant-writing business.

Income Potential for Grant Writers— Writers Making a Small Investment for a Big Financial Return

A grant writer can earn an annual income ranging from $50,000 to $300,000. The income potential depends on a variety of factors, including the level of expertise, area of operation, clients, commissions (if any), and type of funders sought. There is no way to estimate what a grant writer can earn. It depends on whether the grant writer is employed full-time or freelance; whether he or she is a specialist or generalist writer; the number of projects accepted each year; the writer's geographic location; and myriad other considerations. Freelance grant writers can charge an hourly rate that is supported by the marketplace and nearly always earn more than full-time, employed grant writers.

Here are the payment methods commonly accepted by grant writers:

- *By hourly rate.* The rates charged by grant writers vary, depending on their main clientele, level of experience, and success in securing grant approvals. The average hourly rate for a competent grant writer is between $40 and $80. More experienced and capable grant writers can charge rates of $100 per hour or more, while there are less established grant writers who charge between $25 and $50 per hour. The hourly rate and the resultant total fee will be significantly affected by the amount of experience and track record of each grant writer.

- *By project.* Some grant writers prefer to charge on a project basis, after a thorough assessment of the full range and scope of the job. Depending on the length and complexity of the grant document, project fees can range anywhere from $1,000 to $10,000. It is up to the grant writer to decide whether to choose different rates based on the source of grant, e.g., a lower rate for grant applications to be submitted to a foundation or corporation, and a higher rate if the applicant is seeking state or federal grants.

- *Per diem.* Grant consulting firms offer their services per day. In such cases, they charge a standard daily rate that may vary between $500 and $2,000.

Stat Fact

Grant-writing fees vary enormously, from $20 an hour for less experienced writers to $150 per hour for experienced ones. Some charge on a contract basis. Typical rates are $1,250 per diem or $10,000 per government proposal prepared by consulting firms.

- *By commission*. Some grant writers are paid based on a certain percentage of the grant that is awarded. In this arrangement, compensation is tied to the grant writer's success in securing the grant and may be between 1 and 5 percent of the total grant awarded.

A Word about
Grant Writing vs. Fundraising

Grant writing and fundraising are two different things, although a grant writer can also be a fundraiser and vice versa. A fundraiser is a person on staff who is assigned to general fundraising duties, one of which may be grant writing. Fundraising duties also can include nurturing long-term donors; developing candidates and plans for bequests; planning and executing fundraising events or speaker series; managing a database of donors; developing year-end and midyear letter campaigns; and other similar responsibilities.

Becoming a fundraiser or fundraising consultant enhances your ability to get a job as a grant writer, as these roles cover a larger spectrum of raising funds. The job of a fundraiser generally is created only if an organization is planning a complex project and needs to raise a large amount of money.

Most professional fundraisers work for a nonprofit organization, either on staff or on a consultant basis. They do the bread-and-butter work of raising money from private, corporate, and government sources. Usually, fundraisers who are on the staff of a nonprofit are called "development officers." An independent fundraiser goes by the professional term "fundraising counsel."

While many executive directors of nonprofits can and have written grants, they often become too busy with the other requirements of their jobs and grant writing becomes a skill sought from an outside source, such as a professional grant writer. Professional grant writers, as a general rule, work for organizations where there is the biggest potential for income, although some will work for individuals on a for-hire basis.

Professional fundraisers usually maintain a staff of researchers and assistants and are accustomed to conducting funding campaigns from start to finish. Most professional fundraisers work with different types of projects and funders,

Stat Fact

The Foundation Center survey conducted in March 2007, indicates that the number-one leading U.S. foundation by asset size is The Bill and Melinda Gates Foundation, with assets totaling $29,153,508,829.

although there are a few who specialize, for example, in government grants.

Traits of a Grant Writer

To become a professional grant writer, you need to develop skills in writing, storytelling, consulting, research, program planning, evaluation, internet marketing, interviewing, public relations, and budgeting. A good grant writer must have many traits. This section lists some of them.

Tip...

Smart Tip

In addition to the qualities that can make a grant idea attractive to funders, there is one crucial factor that can make or break a funding idea. That factor is you: who you are, what experience or knowledge you possess, how you present yourself, and, perhaps most significantly, how much you care about your idea.

Resilience

Grant writers need to be adaptable and flexible, shifting direction based on the applicant, the needs of the community, and the funder. Grant writers also must be able to recover quickly from the inevitable disappointments of the job.

Goal-Setting

One of the best ways to stay motivated is to set goals. You can set different kinds of goals, such as, "I am going to meet three clients today" or "I will double my annual income within the next two years." Goals give you something to aim for. Always aim high.

Research Skills

A savvy grant writer must be able to research for funding sources in an efficient manner. Some directories of funders (see Chapter 4) are thousands of pages long. Browsing through every single page is out of the question and an utter waste of time. A good grant writer must be able to review through the index and find sources that fit a particular need. Research skills also are needed to hunt for statistics for quantifying information.

Tip...

Smart Tip

Remember, success is failure turned inside out. It is when you are hardest hit by grant rejections that you must not quit. Resilience is a smart trait to cultivate in life.

Internet Savvy

Internet research skills are a must for grant writers. As a grant writer, you surf the web frequently looking for special opportunities for your clients or employer. Part of the work of the grant writer is identifying and selecting appropriate potential donors online. More and more funders are going paperless.

Writing and Speaking Communication Skills

Good writing skills are needed to write a good grant proposal, write high-quality publications that build your reputation, and write excellent follow-up reports once funding has been awarded.

Good speaking skills are necessary to bring your work to the attention of people, make a convincing presentation during a site visit, deliver grant-writing workshops, and successfully coordinate the different elements needed to complete foundation grant applications.

Smart Tip

Setting deadlines for your goals is critical. Aim to achieve tomorrow's goals today. Deadlines and time commitments keep you moving forward. Keep one eye on the long-term opportunity while taking care of today. Teach yourself to focus on the important things and to allow the less critical things to take a back seat.

Sound Administrative Skills

Sound administrative skills are needed to handle the application process. From calling a funder to talk about a possible corporation grant to billing a client for completing a 50-page grant proposal, administrative skills are needed to ensure that the job gets done properly.

Human Relations Skills

Beware!

Remember, you are the company you keep. Improving your career as a freelance grant writer may require you to establish healthy associations. Associate with people who affirm your goodness and share your ambitions—not those who may cause you to lose focus and fall by the wayside.

The grant decisions are ultimately made by humans about humans. The person reading the application is a human being, not a robot. Your ability to interact with human beings comes into effect during several phases of the grant application process. Calling funders, on-site visits, and delivering presentations to funders are a few examples where good human relations come into play. With some applications, there may not be a need to interact with a human being at a tangible level, while with others, such interactions may be necessary.

Relationships are crucial to success. An effective grant writer needs to be confident enough to feel comfortable initiating interactions with strangers.

Passion

Believing strongly in your organization's mission can be a contributing factor to your success as a grant writer. Pick a nonprofit with a mission that speaks to both your heart and mind. Not only will your work be more fulfilling, but enthusiasm will spread to those around you. For example, if you feel strongly about addiction recovery, then work with nonprofit counseling centers and detox facilities. Your enthusiasm for sober living will translate into the proposal you are crafting.

Smart Tip

Tip...

Situational factors are all-important to business success. But their importance is dwarfed in comparison to the burning desire that you must have to make your business venture succeed. You can always make changes to your business once you start, but you can't buy burning desire. If it is not there from the start, you are at a severe disadvantage.

Trustworthiness

People want to know they can depend on you before they commit to a lasting relationship, especially one where resources or money is exchanged. Grant writers who use manipulative techniques to secure gifts and grants are not seen as having integrity. Credibility is something you earn over time. It takes time, effort, and situational need to build trust between a grant writer and a client/funder.

Persistence

It takes thick skin to accept rejection as a matter of course and continue advocating for a cause. Grant writers need to be dogged in their efforts and feel challenged, not defeated, by obstacles. If you are timid, in order to be a successful grant writer, you must transform yourself to move forward amid obstacles. This ability affects your grant-writing career and other areas of your life.

Beware!

Working with clients who may misuse grant funds may cost you your job. If you feel suspicious about a particular individual or organization misusing funds, notify the Federal Bureau of Investigation (FBI), the Internal Revenue Service (IRS), or the county government.

Ability to Lead and Follow

A good grant writer must nurture the ability to lead and follow at the same time. When working with a nonprofit that needs funds raised, you set the direction which the grant-seeking process is going to take. You guide the process, orchestrate the players, and motivate the team to move forward. In this role, there is no room for ego. A good grant writer must be able to bridge relationships with many individuals and organizations.

Simultaneously, a good grant writer must be able to follow guidelines set forth by a funder, obey the requirements made by the director of a nonprofit, and follow the current trends in grant seeking.

> **Tip...**
>
> ### Smart Tip
> Good grant writers must be able to take rejection with their chins up. A grant writer shows resiliency when a funder gives a negative response to a project idea, and the grant writer overcomes the objection or shifts focus to another initiative without missing a beat.

Confident

As a grant writer, confidence is key to convincing a funder of your ability to successfully carry out the project. If you are knowledgeable about your field, know your organization and its programs well, and prepare for interactions with prospective donors, your confidence grows significantly. A confident person is not embarrassed by what she does not know and freely admits it. She is aware of her own shortcomings but maintains a sense of purpose.

Allow your organization to stand on its own feet without bringing someone else down.

Multitasker

In order to complete the multiple tasks and responsibilities of a grant writer, you need to juggle many things at once without coming unglued. One of the main measures of successful grant writers is their ability to follow through with peers at the nonprofit as well as with funders and other partners. You must have a continual focus on the overall goal, while attending to the details that allow the project to be successfully developed and implemented.

Organizational skills are important for successful multitasking. You must be organized so you can manage all the required tasks and responsibilities. A grant writer must be able to keep track of grant application deadlines and follow up on submitted applications. It is also essential to keep track of trends in the field as well be aware of changes in the priorities of funding institutions and new funding sources that come onto the scene.

> ### Beware!
> Coating yourself in denial or fake optimism should not be confused with confidence.

Grant Writer's Toolkit

Grant writing is a craft that can be cultivated and mastered in time. Knowing how to use the tools of the trade is key to winning funding. Although there isn't a set procedure for becoming a successful grant writer, some standard rules apply.

Smart Tip

Tip...

The grant proposal demands a different genre of writing. It is not an academic paper, a report, a novel, or a newspaper article. It is a document of persuasion.

Approaching Funders

There are a number of methods of approaching funders:

- Grant proposal
- Personal visit
- Telephone call
- E-mail or fax

The best method of approaching a funder depends on how much money is sought, the grantmaking organization, and the project idea, among other factors. The most common method of approaching funders is through a grant proposal.

The Grant Proposal in a Nutshell

The grant proposal is the umbilical cord connecting a grant writer with potential funders. Through the grant proposal, applicants have the opportunity to persuade the funder to give money.

Learning how to write persuasive grant proposals is key to winning funding. A well-written, cohesive proposal can bring in money and, in some cases, donated goods and services. Figure 1.1 on page 10 shows the main elements of a grant proposal and what information should be included. Chapter 6 discusses grant proposals in detail.

Tip...

Smart Tip

A beginning grant writer is strongly advised to start with private foundation and not federal grant proposals. Because the federal government offers large sums of money, proposals for these grants are much more competitive than those grants issued by private foundations. In addition, most foundation proposals are fairly easy and straightforward to write.

Researching Funders

Knowing where to look for grant funders is key. Researching funders who are likely to provide financial support for your work requires

Figure 1.1: Main Elements of a Grant Proposal

Category	Information to Include
Proposal summary	Briefly state how the project will be implemented and the expected results; include your total budget, timeline, and the amount of your request.
Statement of problem or need	Explain the problems you are going to address; outline current resources that address this problem and identify gaps in those resources; identify how your proposal fills these gaps.
Project goals and objectives	Identify the specific goals you are trying to achieve and the measurable milestones you will reach to meet those goals
Methodology	Describe the actions you will take to achieve your goals, the steps that must be taken to achieve success, as well as when and where the actions will take place.
Evaluation	Explain how you will determine whether you achieved your goals, any measures in place to evaluate your progress, as well as any records and information that will be used in the evaluation.
Budget	Include the amount of money you are requesting, any calculations for specific items for which funds are being requested, and the time line during which funds will be used.

time, patience, and perseverance. Always remember to look at the funder's current guidelines. Grant profiles, contact information, and funding criteria change frequently. The internet is an excellent source to look for funders. You are likely to find the most current information available online, simply because web sites are easier to update than print publications. Chapter 4 fleshes out prospect research in extensive detail.

Identify the Problem, Propose a Solution

Because funders want their money to make a positive difference in society, they want to see applications that solve a problem or address a need—locally, nationally, or internationally. But the funder also has legitimate business considerations to weigh. Put yourself in the funder's shoes and answer the question, "What's in it for me?" All funders want to know both how your project helps them meet their goals and how it adds value to the well-being of the community. Use your grant proposal to show, in plain terms, what positive differences your idea has on society and to provide a glimpse of what the situation would look like if your project is not funded. By identifying a pressing problem and proposing a solution, show how an investment in your project has positive effects—for the funder and for society.

Focus on results. Show how your idea can improve the conditions of people or, in some cases, animals and the environment; make your idea convincing, important, and immediate. Funders look for projects that produce a clear outcome and lasting benefits. Using data to define needs and track progress toward outcomes is a good way to show the funder you are serious about results.

2

Who Needs
Grants?

Nonprofit organizations account for the largest percentage of grant seekers. These organizations operate as charities and usually offer promise of helping their communities at the local, national, and sometimes international levels. Grants are a key source of support for many nonprofit organizations, particularly new ones.

Stat Fact

More than 90 percent of foundation grants are awarded to nonprofit organizations with 501(c)(3) status. There are more than 200,000 nonprofits in the United States alone. In some developing countries, nonprofits are known as nongovernmental organizations (NGOs), and each NGO relies on a grant writer to craft proposals.

Grants for Nonprofits

Nearly all nonprofit organizations must seek grants to develop new programs or sustain operations. In the smaller nonprofit agencies, the task of grant seeking is often assigned to the executive director. Larger organizations often hire a fund development officer to perform the task. As executive directors of nonprofits have become busier and busier, the need for professional grant-writing services has grown rapidly. On occasion, program directors are assigned responsibility for seeking grants to support the organization's programs or ideas. In many cases, a nonprofit's board of directors mandates that staff pursue a specified number of grants or raise a specific amount of money through grant writing in any given year.

Internet fundraising has changed the way grant writers operate. Instead of being physically present at a nonprofit and reporting for work every morning, grant writers now can work for several organizations simultaneously from their homes at the click of a button. A grant writer based out of Connecticut can work for a nonprofit in Hawaii or in Japan.

To apply for grants, small nonprofit organizations must decide whether to educate existing staff in proposal preparation, recruit a local volunteer with solid writing skills, or hire a fundraising consultant. Instead, most opt to hire a professional grant writer.

When nonprofits open their doors to the world of grants, they gain several benefits:

- Increase their budget
- Increase their reputation as a charitable organization in the community and at national levels
- Provide individuals with financial support to succeed
- Obtain operational support
- Provide communities with opportunities to pursue their goals

A well-prepared proposal can build an organization's credibility with funders and bring in lots of money. The elements of the grant proposal to be included in the application are the same for individual and nonprofit applicants. Nonprofit applicants, however, have to include

Tip...

Smart Tip

In a typical mid-sized city in the United States, there are thousands of nonprofit organizations and only two or three professional grant writers.

appendices such as a letter of tax exemption, audited financial statements, and Board member affiliations. Often, on-site meetings with potential funders are also a necessity for non-profits.

Grants for Individuals

Individuals qualify to apply for funding on their own merit, without the backing of an institution. Private foundations and family trusts are more likely to award grants to individuals than the federal government. Private foundation awards may be small, but they are easier to get than federal government grants. The level of difficulty and required length of individual grant applications vary. Some funders may require a simple letter of inquiry while others may have a more complex application process.

Grants to individuals are awarded for various purposes. Two of the fields are discussed in detail because they are popular categories with individual applicants. Some of the most common are:

- Higher education
- Emergency living expenses
- Publishing books
- Conducting research
- Starting a small business
- Humanitarian work in developing countries

Grants for Higher Education

There are two basic categories of student financial aid: need based (when students do not have sufficient financial resources to pay for their education and careers) and non-need based (often referred to as merit-based aid and frequently awarded to students in recognition of special skills, talents, or academic abilities). See Chapter 4 for listings of places that award grants to students for college tuition, graduate research, scholarships, and other educational funding.

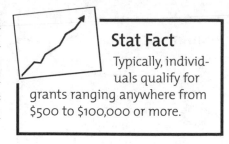

Stat Fact

Typically, individuals qualify for grants ranging anywhere from $500 to $100,000 or more.

Emergency Grants

Individuals may qualify for emergency expenses to help with day-to-day living expenses, including:

- Health insurance
- Hospital bills
- Loan and debt payments
- Recovery from events such as tornadoes, hurricanes, floods, and tsunami
- Rent/mortgage
- Medical bills
- Addiction recovery expenses (i.e., rehabilitation for alcoholic treatment, substance abuse treatment, psychotherapy, detoxification, and sober-living counseling)
- Food and clothing
- Physical therapy
- Child-care and baby-sitting expenses
- Insurance
- Utility bills

See Chapter 4 for contact listing of places that award emergency grants to individuals.

Types of Grants

Grants fall into a myriad of categories, but funders often define the type of money they distribute in one of the following ways:

- *Project grant.* A project grant supports a particular project or program of an individual or organization. For example, a project grant could pay a university to conduct research on asthma or to organize a summer music festival in the community.

- *General operating grant.* A general operating grant is one made to an organization or individual to cover operating expenses for an ongoing program or project. This type of broad-based, unrestricted grant can cover anything from rent to the electricity bill to staff salaries or artists' fees. In other words, general operating grants provide funding for anything needed to keep the project going.

- *Capital or endowment grant.* Funds from these types of grants are used for remodeling and renovation, supplies and equipment, construction; building expansion, and the purchase of land or equipment.

- *Restricted grant.* A restricted grant covers one specified part of a project, such as the fee for a musical score for a theater production being presented by an arts council.

- *General purpose grant.* A general purpose grant is a broad-based grant that is not restricted to any particular purpose and that assists with the ongoing work of an organization. General purpose grants generally are given only to organizations. An example is a $50,000 grant given to the Red Cross to support its work in developing countries.

- *Start-up funds or seed money.* Start-up funds or seed money is given to help an organization or individual start a new program or project. Seed money can cover salaries, operating expenses, and other expenses necessary to start a new venture, such as a new business.

- *Challenge grant.* A challenge grant is an award that will be paid by a contributing organization if the grant seeker is able to raise a specified amount of matching funds. For example, a foundation will give a $30,000 challenge grant to a nonprofit if it also raises $30,000 through another grant.

- *Matching grant.* A matching grant is similar to a challenge grant. A funder gives money to match funds granted by another organization. For example, the Ford Foundation may decide to match a $70,000 grant made by the Hearst Foundation to help fund a research program at Clark University.

- *Re-grant program.* A re-grant program is an arrangement whereby a private foundation or a government agency gives funds to a nonprofit organization, which in turn uses these funds to administer a grant program—soliciting proposals and giving grants—usually on a local level.

- *Special projects.* Special projects grants generally are restricted to starting a new program within a limited time frame.

Smart Tip

Tip...

Examples of in-kind contributions include computers, fax machines, office equipment, office space, exhibition space, supplies for mailings, or any other kind of donation aside from direct cash gifts.

- *Research*. Research grants are offered mostly for scientific, academic, and university work.
- *Student aid*. These types of funds come in the form of scholarships, awards, and fellowships to help students at the high school and college levels.
- *In-kind contribution or service*. An in-kind contribution or service is a contribution to an organization or individual that might consist of materials, equipment, property, or services of some kind. This is sometimes called a noncash grant.
- *Technical assistance*. Technical assistance is aid in the form of free consulting services that are offered to nonprofit organizations and sometimes to individuals. Donated services may include fund raising or budgeting assistance, financial or legal advice, or computer training. Corporations may offer technical assistance as a part of their funding program.
- *Fellowships*. Fellowships are grants for educational studies or research, usually at the graduate or postgraduate level. Fellowships always are granted to individuals, although the funds may be channeled through a sponsor. The term "scholarships" strictly applies to undergraduates, although it is sometimes used loosely for both undergraduate and graduate grants.
- *Awards and prizes*. Awards and prizes are grants given on a competitive basis for specific accomplishments or achievements. Awards and prizes are typically given to individuals.

In general, funding is allocated to the following types of grant projects, from highest to lowest, according to data from the Foundation Center for 1998–2001:

- Program support (between 42.6 percent and 45.7 percent)
- Capital or endowment projects (between 19 percent and 24.3 percent)
- General operating support (between 13.7 percent and 19 percent)
- Research (between 8.5 percent and 11.4 percent)
- Student aid (between 5 percent and 11.3 percent)

A nonprofit organization approaching a grantmaker must have most of the following attributes:

- Strong and recent data to support the need for the project
- An experienced project manager
- A history of fiscal responsibility
- A response that clearly addresses the identified need
- Collaboration with others in the community
- Community member involvement in identifying the problem and the solution

3

Types of Funders

Understanding the distribution patterns of foundations, corporations, and federal funders can help you become a thriving grant writer. The agendas of foundations, corporations, government agencies, private individuals, and nonprofits vary widely.

An important element of a nonprofit's comprehensive fundraising strategy is often grants from corporations and foundations. After all, these organizations are primarily structured to make charitable contributions and exist mainly to allocate funds to nonprofit organizations.

By partnering with a nonprofit, a corporation or foundation can achieve its goals, such as increasing knowledge, providing programs for the disadvantaged, and economic development. These partnerships can be mutually beneficial when the interests of the nonprofit fit well with a funder's goals.

Beware!

Relying on just one funding source may be detrimental to your grant-seeking efforts. The old adage of not putting all your eggs in one basket certainly applies to raising sufficient funds. Create a healthy mix of foundation, corporate, and federal grant applications.

Independent, Community, Operating, and Family Foundations

A foundation is an organization formed either as a nonprofit corporation or charitable trust. Its main purpose is to make grants to unrelated organizations or individuals for scientific, cultural, religious, or other charitable purposes. Foundations are either private (meaning the foundation derives the majority of its funds from one source, an individual, a family, or a corporation) or public (meaning the foundation receives its funds from many sources and must continue to raise funds through a variety of means in order to keep its public status). Both individuals and organizations qualify to apply for grants from either private or public foundations.

Stat Fact

In many cases, foundations and corporate giving programs are bound by tax law to give money to nonprofits. In fact, charitable private foundations are required to pay out, through grant making, 5 percent of the total corpus (endowment plus earnings) each year. Your job as the grant writer is to discover corporations and foundations that share your interests and want to invest in your programs.

Whether private or public, there are several types of foundations: independent, community, operating, and family. These foundation types differ in their character, intent, creation, structure, and revenue streams. Understanding foundations' similarities and differences can result in effective grant seeking. Remember, the agendas of foundations, corporations, government agencies, private individuals, and nonprofits vary widely and it's your job as a grant writer to find good matches.

Independent Foundations

The majority of foundations in existence today are independent foundations, which are private entities set up to distribute grants to tax-exempt organizations. These types of foundations generally are funded by individuals or families through one of two ways:

1. Endowment—where the income earned from investment of the principal is used to make grants; or

2. Periodic contributions—where living donors contribute to the fund, using the foundation as a pass-through for their giving.

The most well-known independent foundations are the "Big Daddy" foundations: Ford Foundation, Rockefeller Foundation, and William Randolph Hearst Foundation. These have been set up by major philanthropists and wealthy business-people to help better society. They give away large sums of money every year. Independent foundations are usually administered by attorneys or bank trust depart-ments and are often named for the original donors.

In most cases, giving categories are established by independent foundations. They are very specific about how they want the monies allocated. Independent foundations range in size from very small, such as a $10,000 endowment, to those with hundreds of millions of dollars in assets. ("Big Daddy" foundations give away large sums of money every year.)

Community Foundations

Community foundations are locally or regionally focused. They accumulate assets through a number of donors, establishing an endowment that is managed independently. A community foundation uses the income from the endowment to make grants. Nonprofits with local interests are more likely to receive funding from a community foundation than from a national foundation because of less competition, and there is a more direct link between the donor's local interests and the community-based organization applying for a grant.

Community foundations are a great exam-ple of strength in numbers. Usually established by one or two donors in a community, these foundations broaden their effectiveness by per-suading other successful individuals to con-tribute through direct donations, legacy gifts, or annual donations.

Stat Fact
There are more than 2,000 cor-porate foundations in the United States.

Top Community Foundations

The Foundation Center survey, conducted in March, 2007, lists the Greater Kansas City Community Foundation as the number-one U.S. foundation in total giving. Its total giving at the end of the 2005 fiscal year was $140,702,000. The New York Community Trust followed a close second, with a total giving of $136,970,963 in fiscal year 2005.

Operating Foundations

Operating foundations are classified by the Internal Revenue Service (IRS) as such because they spend at least 85 percent of their income supporting their own programs. They generally do not make grants but exist to conduct research and programs.

Categories of Giving

Foundations typically give in the following categories:

○ Capital support
○ Continuing support
○ Endowments
○ Fellowships and scholarships
○ Matching or challenge grants
○ Operating support
○ Program support
○ Research

Legally separate from other types of foundations, operating foundations enjoy a more favorable tax status. They raise funds, are governed by a board of directors, and employ a professional staff to direct and carry out programs.

Family Foundations

Family foundations are generally established by one or two donors, typically an entrepreneur, siblings, or a married couple. Founded to ensure that future generations continue to practice philanthropy, family foundations are set up so that the endowment upholds values the founders believe are important. Most founders are successful entrepreneurs who want to use their fortunes to support the communities in which they and their families live. In return for their generosity, founders receive substantial tax benefits from the federal government.

Corporations

Corporate philanthropy is about giving away money. Clearly, businesses must see a benefit to their giving. Many corporate grant makers have

Beware!
Corporate philanthropy is sometimes referred to as "enlightened self-interest," as some companies may engage in philanthropic activities to promote an agenda. For example, a computer manufacturer may donate computers to local schools as a business strategy to promote its brand.

developed philanthropic strategies in line with their business values. Corporations also may look for opportunities to expose potential customers to their products or services. Sometimes with corporate funders there may be a hidden, vested interest in

Top Corporate Foundations

The Foundation Center survey, conducted in March, 2007, indicates that the number-one U.S. corporation by asset size is The Wells Fargo Foundation, with assets totaling $554,108,137 at the end of fiscal year December 31, 2005. Following closely in second place is the Alcoa Foundation with assets totaling $550,363,160.

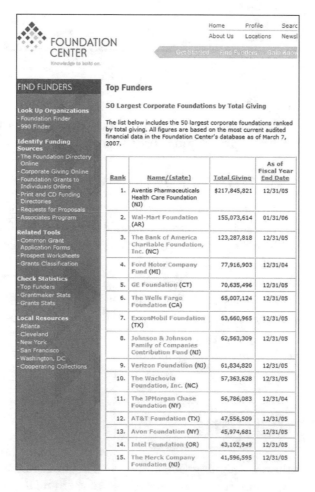

Top Funders

50 Largest Corporate Foundations by Total Giving

The list below includes the 50 largest corporate foundations ranked by total giving. All figures are based on the most current audited financial data in the Foundation Center's database as of March 7, 2007.

Rank	Name/(state)	Total Giving	As of Fiscal Year End Date
1.	Aventis Pharmaceuticals Health Care Foundation (NJ)	$217,845,821	12/31/05
2.	Wal-Mart Foundation (AR)	155,073,614	01/31/06
3.	The Bank of America Charitable Foundation, Inc. (NC)	123,287,818	12/31/05
4.	Ford Motor Company Fund (MI)	77,916,903	12/31/04
5.	GE Foundation (CT)	70,635,496	12/31/05
6.	The Wells Fargo Foundation (CA)	65,007,124	12/31/05
7.	ExxonMobil Foundation (TX)	63,660,965	12/31/05
8.	Johnson & Johnson Family of Companies Contribution Fund (NJ)	62,563,309	12/31/05
9.	Verizon Foundation (NJ)	61,834,820	12/31/05
10.	The Wachovia Foundation, Inc. (NC)	57,363,628	12/31/05
11.	The JPMorgan Chase Foundation (NY)	56,786,083	12/31/04
12.	AT&T Foundation (TX)	47,556,509	12/31/05
13.	Avon Foundation (NY)	45,974,681	12/31/05
14.	Intel Foundation (OR)	43,102,949	12/31/05
15.	The Merck Company Foundation (NJ)	41,596,595	12/31/05

their philanthropy, which the funders may or may not disclose readily.

Corporate foundations are subject to the same rules and regulations as other private foundations and are legally separate from the corporation with which they are affiliated, although their distributions are usually dependent on the company's profits. In order to fund the foundation, corporations take a portion of their profits and put it into a dedicated fund for philanthropy. The corporate foundation can legally support areas of strategic interest as long as the corporation does not profit directly from its foundation's grant making.

Corporate foundations generally are most interested in helping organizations where their employees live. For example, Cessna may establish a funding program in Wichita, Kansas, to pay for employees' childrens' college educations. Or, corporate foundations missions may state that they want to improve the quality of life for all citizens in the communities where they operate as a means of improving their own employees' lives.

Corporate philanthropists realize that a good program can accomplish many things, including:

- Fulfilling social and civic responsibilities
- Strengthening the communities in which the company operates
- Establishing good relationships with the surrounding community
- Improving customer relations
- Inproving employee morale
- Increasing business and profits

Cash is a common form of corporate philanthropy. Direct cash donations vary from a few thousand to several million dollars. However, there are other ways that corporations help nonprofits.

- *In-kind services*. Some corporations donate employee time and talent. In such cases, nonprofits benefit by not incurring overhead costs. Examples of in-kind services include printing or accounting services. A recent trend has been to combine cash grants, in-kind contributions, and employee volunteer services when seeking to help a nonprofit. Volunteers can provide valuable services that would otherwise tap into an organization's resources.

- *Executive loans.* Large corporations may have programs where an executive's time is loaned to a nonprofit.

- *Matching gifts.* Many corporations match—to a certain dollar amount—their employees' financial donations, thereby leveraging additional dollars for the charitable organization. Companies also are beginning to match volunteer hours with cash, making it even more lucrative for employees to support the organizations they care about.

- *Product donations.* Corporations gain from donating new or used products. They get certain tax advantages and, in the case of used products, can save money in the storage and disposal of these products.

Government Funding

Federal government grants are where the money is and where the work is. Federal government grants are meant to launch big programs. That is why awards can range from less than $10,000 to several million dollars. Government funders have the responsibility of giving away taxpayers' money. As with other areas of government spending, many checks and balances have been set up to protect these public funds, which originate from the local, state, and federal levels. Government grants are often issued in the form of contracts, which are essentially the delegation of government responsibility to a third-party organization. The government often gives multiyear grants, which provide a predictable source of funding for several years. For example, a public hospital may receive a $500,000 grant payable over two years to build an asthma research facility.

Local, State, and Pass-Through Funds

Government grants are tax dollars that are redistributed to programs in the community. As such, these grants can be made by any entity that collects taxes (i.e., federal, state, and even local

Help from the Feds

Federal assistance programs come in a variety of types. Loans, direct money payments, exchanging of goods and information, and training support are some off them. The type of federal assistance program depends on the issuing organization, type of government contract, and the need of the applicant, among other factors. Federal assistance programs are generally categorized as follows:

- Advisory services and counseling
- Direct loan
- Direct payments (grants)
- Project grants
- Sale, exchange, or donation of property and goods
- Use of property, facilities, and equipment

city or county governments). Overall, the government grant-seeking process is similar to the process in the foundation and corporate world, perhaps just a little bit more intense.

- *Local government funds.* Local governments refer to a city, township, county, regional coordinating body, or other such mediums. Local governments rarely have grant opportunities, and those that do provide only limited programs. Local governments are more likely to issue requests for proposals (RFPs) soliciting bids for work to be completed.

- *State government funds.* Grants from the state are among the easiest to apply for and receive. The state is likely knowledgeable about a community's situation and any problems occurring while also being large enough to provide grants in sufficient amounts to address the situation.

Applicants can find state grant opportunities in nearly the same way as they find federal government grants: by going from department to department. Most states have a web site that lists departments, and pages within each department contain information about their funding programs.

- *Pass-through funds.* State or federal governments occasionally provide pass-through funds to a nonprofit organization. To receive pass-through funds, the local agency usually acts as a type of "project manager," receiving some compensation for reviewing the grant proposals, distributing the grant dollars, and ensuring all reports and evaluations are submitted on time to the grant agency. The pass-through agent is likely to be your local government, one of the local nonprofits, or your community foundation.

▲

Request for Proposals (RFPs)

Typically, there are three ways nonprofits receive grants:

1. In response to a Request for Proposals (RFP)
2. In response to a broad agency announcement (BAA)
3. Due to "cold calling"

When it is an RFP or BAA, an organization receives a request for proposals that clearly outlines the types of projects the funder is seeking and the requirements for each project. A "cold call" is when an organization approaches a foundation, describes the need identified in the community that is not being met by any other agency, and tells what can be done to make a positive difference. In all three situations the funder is in the "giving" end while the nonprofit applicant is in the "receiving" end. The funder has all the control in the decision-making process.

When applying for a RFP the grant writer must examine the criteria for eligibility and determine whether the nonprofit is a good fit for the project. The grant writer's strategy is to emphasize how a specific grant request can help fulfill the funder's own mission. In all cases, the grant writer must follow the instructions and the outline provided either in the RFP or in the funder's guidelines.

Each section of the grant proposal carries a certain number of points, which refer to the grading system in federal applications. They are then totaled, and the highest ones are awarded grants. So, by knowing the number of points awarded for each section of the narrative, applicants are able to strengthen their applications accordingly.

The proposal elements (as described in Chapter 6) are the same for a RFP as they are for any other grant proposal.

Each RFP contains the following information:

- A purpose statement
- The issuing agency/department
- The criteria for the program, including eligibility requirements
- The total grants available and range of prospective grant awards
- Statements that must be signed by the applicant
- The deadline
- Mailing instructions
- An outline of proposal content
- Any points available for each section of the narrative
- A rubric (a chart of judging criteria and scoring) or other selection criteria for judges
- An application kit containing budget forms, cover sheets, and assurances
- Appendices/documents, resources, call for reviewers, etc.

After you find a RFP online, the first thing to read is the purpose of the project: what does the funder hope to accomplish with its money? If the stated purpose matches the purpose or mission of your program, good. Next, look at the list of qualified applicants. The list of qualified applicants mean that the agency issuing the RFP specified certain criteria that they want to see in their applicants. For instance, some grants call for the applicant to be a community arts organization or a local education agency. If your organization does not qualify, don't apply. Save yourself time, energy, and resources, and keep looking to find a RFP from a source that is more likely to fund your request.

If your organization meets the RFP requirements, check the deadline. Is there enough time to complete an application or will it be done at the eleventh hour? Reading the grant narrative will help you estimate the work load and degree of difficulty, and determine if there is enough time to complete the application.

Next, consider the funding allocation, average amount of awards, and probable number of projects. When the average grant award is several hundred thousand or million dollars, you can be sure that hundreds of qualified organizations will apply. If the department expects to award only 20 new grants each year, you must calculate the odds of your project being one of them.

Often RFPs are issued for programs that require a certain local match. Match requirements vary, and the RFP will describe what qualifies. For instance, a 40 percent local cash match means that you must have already made commitments to secure part of the money needed for a project *before* applying for the remaining portion. If the RFP states that in-kind money qualifies, you can gather a portion of the required match in donated space; staff time for coordinating or attending meetings; existing furnishings and computer equipment; and other items that are part of your organization's budget. An example is a performing arts organizations may receive notification from the National Endowment for Humanities.

Carefully study the sustainability requirements set forth by the RFP. Some federal grants require that an organization apply for a four-year decreasing amount grant. For instance, the grant may provide 75 percent of funding needed for the first year, 60 percent for the second year, 40 percent for the third year, and 20 percent for the fourth. In this case, the applicant organization must commit to providing an increasing amount of its own money to continuing the program for the four-year term of the grant.

When you download an RFP, be sure to bookmark the web site so you can check it once

Smart Tip

Tip...

Governments cannot be solicited for funds.
Instead, you must rely on matching your project with an appropriate RFP. Watch for RFPs not only from the most obvious departments—such as Department of Education grants for school districts—but also from other departments.

or twice during the time you are writing the application. You will find latest news, such as an extended deadline, clarification of the RFP based on questions from others, or changes in the level or funding since the RFP was issued.

Where Do You Find RFPs?

You, or the executive director of your organization, may already be on a mailing list for appropriate RFPs. For instance school districts receive most announcements issued by the Department of Education; large mental health agencies are notified by the Department of Health and Human Services; and police departments will be given notice of grants available from the Department of Justice. As you develop these larger nonprofits as long-term clients, they will begin to send you the RFPs and ask your opinion about whether they are qualified to pursue the grant program or if the proposed program is appropriate for their needs.

If you are working as a freelance grant writer, you can review RFPs on your own and call your clients and potential clients when you think that one of the RFPs matches their requirements. It can take a while to locate different departments and agencies that issue RFPs. So be sure to bookmark sites that you know you will want to return to.

RFPs are published by each federal agency and can be found on individual web sites. You can also go to your local congressional representative's office and ask to review the office copy of the Federal Register. The Federal Register contains all proposed grant opportunities for the upcoming year, regardless of the issuing federal department. The register is published or updated annually but is not distributed. Instead, a one- or two page announcement is mailed to pre-established mailing lists approximately 90 to 120 days before the grant deadline. The announcement contains a brief description of the program, its federal register number, the requesting department, a list of legal entities that may apply, the web address for the full RFP, and an application or a telephone number to request an application package. The register also contains information about any grant seeker workshops or conferences that will take place and where they will be held.

Finding
Grants

Uncle Sam gives away billions of dollars in grants every year. Federal grants are competitive and offer anywhere between $1,000 and several million dollars per applicant. There are more than 26 federal grant-making agencies offering thousands of grant programs. This section lists resources for researching federal grant programs.

Grants.gov

Grants.gov (www.grants.gov) is your source to search and apply for federal grants. The U.S. Department of Health and Human Services is the managing partner for Grants.gov. While you do not have to register with Grants.gov to search for grant opportunities, you do need to register to apply for a grant. The registration process takes between three and five business days. You also can use Grants.gov to track grant applications once they have been submitted.

Stat Fact

Grants.gov allows organizations to electronically search and apply for more than $400 billion in federal grants. All discretionary grants offered by the 26 Federal grant-making agencies can be found on this site. Go to www.grants.gov and click on "Find Grant Opportunities."

Catalog of Federal Domestic Assistance

The *Catalog of Federal Domestic Assistance* (CFDA) lists federal grant opportunities. The online version (at www.cfda.gov) gives you access to a database of all federal

Sample CFDA Web Page

Here is a sample CFDA listing of fields in which grants are available. There are hundreds more.

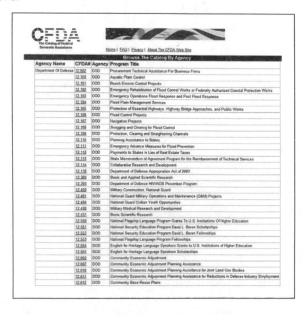

programs available to state and local governments; federally recognized American Indian tribal governments; territories (and possessions) of the United States; domestic public, quasi-public, and private for-profit and nonprofit organizations and institutions; specialized groups; and individuals. After you find the program you want to apply through, contact the office that administers the program for instructions. For valuable tips on how to write proposals for the federal government, read the online section "Writing Grant Proposals" under the "Features" menu.

Federal Register

Published by the Office of the Federal Register, National Archives and Records Administration (NARA), the Federal Register is an official daily publication that, in part, provides notices of federal funding availability, announces grant opportunities, and gives general information about grant programs. The Federal Register also contains requests for proposals (RFPs) issued in a given year by all federal departments.

FirstGov

The first U.S. government web site (at www.firstgov.gov) provides easy, one-stop access to federal government information and services. Click on "Benefits and Grants" to find an alphabetical list of grants awarded in different fields.

USA Government Grants

At www.usagovernmentgrants.org, grants are listed under topics such as housing grants, college grants, personal grants, and women's grants. There is a fee for obtaining a listing of funders.

Grant Directory Publications

Good old-fashioned books provide valuable information on where to look for grants. If you are buying grant directories, always make sure to buy the current edition. Grant-writing books are shelved in the fundraising section of most bookstores. At the library, grant directories are shelved in the reference section and generally cannot be taken from the premises. Ask the reference librarian where to locate the grant directories.

Foundation Grants to Individuals

Phyllis Edelson's *Foundation Grants to Individuals*, (New York: The Foundation Center, 2007) provides a comprehensive listing of private foundations, some of which provide financial assistance to individuals. Areas of funding are categorized as follows: educational support; restricted to company employees; general welfare; arts and cultural support; and restricted to graduates or students of specific schools. For each foundation, it provides the application address, any limitations, financial data, the EIN (employer identification number), foundation type, and application information.

Directory of Grants in the Humanities 2005/2006

The *Directory of Grants in the Humanities* (Phoenix, Arizona: Oryx Publishing, 2007) contains brief descriptions of more than 4,000 funding programs that support research and performance in literature, language, linguistics, history, anthropology, philosophy, ethics, religion, as well as the fine and performing arts, including painting, dance, photography, sculpture, music, drama, crafts, folklore, and mime. Programs fund research, travel, internships, fellowships, dissertation support, conferences, and performances. Each listing includes deadline dates, contact name and address, restrictions, and amount of money available.

The Foundation Reporter

The Foundation Reporter (Cincinnati, Ohio: Taft Publications) is widely used research tool that includes 1,000 of the top foundations in the country that have at least $10 million in assets and give $500,000 in charitable giving each year.

National Directory of Corporate Giving

This is a comprehensive source of information on more than 3,600 corporate grant makers across the country. The *National Directory of Corporate Giving* (New York: Foundation Center, 2007) also provides information on more than 6,500 grants awarded and corporate profiles of the businesses

Stat Fact
According to the *Chronicle of Philanthropy,* the Herb Ritts Foundation gave $2.5 million to the Museum of Fine Arts in Boston, Massachusetts in 2007.

including their location, mission, financials, business interests, and names of high-ranking corporate officials.

Annual Register of Grant Support: A Directory of Funding Sources

This book by R.R. Bowker (Medford, New Jersey: Information Today, Inc., 2005) provides information on more obscure sources, such as unions and associations. The register provides eligibility requirements, contact information, grant ranges, funder priorities, and deadlines for more than 3,500 grant sources.

Grants Register 2005: The Complete Guide to Postgraduate Funding Worldwide

This is a prospect research tool that contains information about private and public funding sources for domestic and international grant. *The Grants Register* (New York: Palgrave Macmillan, 2005) provides information about:

- Scholarships
- Fellowships and research grants
- Exchange opportunities and travel grants
- Grants for artistic and scientific projects
- Competitions, prizes, and honoraria
- Professional and vocational awards
- Special awards

The Foundation Center

Established in 1956, the Foundation Center (http://fdncenter.org) is dedicated to serving grant seekers, grant makers, researchers, policymakers, the media, and the general public. The center's mission is to support and improve philanthropy by promoting public understanding of the field and helping grant seekers to succeed. Figure 4.1 on page 36 shows the top ten U.S. foundations by asset size for 2005.

The Foundation Center provides education about and training for the grant-seeking process. Some of the Foundation Center's available tools include:

- *Foundation finder.* Users can search by name for basic financial and contact information for more than 70,000 private and community foundations in the United States.

▲

- *Grant makers' web sites*. Four distinct directories provide annotated links to grant makers' web sites organized by grant-maker type, allowing users to search or browse summaries of the collected sites.
- *Sector search*. A specialty search engine indexes every page of useful grant writing related sites on the internet.
- *990-PF search*. This is a searchable database of the 990-PF tax returns filed with the Internal Revenue Service by 60,000 private foundations. Tax record's listings of giving patterns, award amounts, board members, and so forth can help

Top Ten U.S. Foundations by Asset Size for 2005

FOUNDATION CENTER
Knowledge to build on.

Home   Profile   Searc
About Us   Locations   Newsl

Get Started · Find Funders · Gain Know

FIND FUNDERS

Look Up Organizations
- Foundation Finder
- 990 Finder

Identify Funding Sources
- The Foundation Directory Online
- Corporate Giving Online
- Foundation Grants to Individuals Online
- Print and CD Funding Directories
- Requests for Proposals
- Associates Program

Related Tools
- Common Grant Application Forms
- Prospect Worksheets
- Grants Classification

Check Statistics
- Top Funders
- Grantmaker Stats
- Grants Stats

Local Resources
- Atlanta
- Cleveland
- New York
- San Francisco
- Washington, DC
- Cooperating Collections

Top Funders

50 Largest Corporate Foundations by Total Giving

The list below includes the 50 largest corporate foundations ranked by total giving. All figures are based on the most current audited financial data in the Foundation Center's database as of March 7, 2007.

Rank	Name/(state)	Total Giving	As of Fiscal Year End Date
1.	Aventis Pharmaceuticals Health Care Foundation (NJ)	$217,845,821	12/31/05
2.	Wal-Mart Foundation (AR)	155,073,614	01/31/06
3.	The Bank of America Charitable Foundation, Inc. (NC)	123,287,818	12/31/05
4.	Ford Motor Company Fund (MI)	77,916,903	12/31/04
5.	GE Foundation (CT)	70,635,496	12/31/05
6.	The Wells Fargo Foundation (CA)	65,007,124	12/31/05
7.	ExxonMobil Foundation (TX)	63,660,965	12/31/05
8.	Johnson & Johnson Family of Companies Contribution Fund (NJ)	62,563,309	12/31/05
9.	Verizon Foundation (NJ)	61,834,820	12/31/05
10.	The Wachovia Foundation, Inc. (NC)	57,363,628	12/31/05
11.	The JPMorgan Chase Foundation (NY)	56,786,083	12/31/04
12.	AT&T Foundation (TX)	47,556,509	12/31/05
13.	Avon Foundation (NY)	45,974,681	12/31/05
14.	Intel Foundation (OR)	43,102,949	12/31/05
15.	The Merck Company Foundation (NJ)	41,596,595	12/31/05

you decide if a foundation is a good match with your needs. To access these tools, log on to http://fdncenter.org.

Newsletters

Newsletters—often warehouses for grants research—are published by grants associations, resource centers, foundations, and nonprofit organizations. By subscribing, you can stay up-to-date on current job openings, fundraising events, and RFPs.

Foundation Center Newsletters

Foundation Center Newsletters are free at www.fdncenter.org/newsletters/index.html and include *Philanthropy News Digest*, *RFP Bulletin*, *Job Corner Alert*, *News from the Foundation Center*, and news from various libraries. The *RFP Bulletin* directly links you to news about funding opportunities, while other publications keep you up-to-date on trends, provide research tips, and ultimately make you a more effective researcher.

Foundation News and Commentary

This bimonthly publication reports on current developments in the grant-making industry with news, feature profiles, and special reports. *Foundation News and Commentary* also includes classified advertising. It is published by the *Council on Foundations* and is a subscription newsletter. Log on to www.foundationnews.org for more information.

The Chronicle of Philanthropy

The *Chronicle of Philanthropy* is a biweekly publication that informs about trends and issues in the nonprofit world; updates grant-making activities; and features profiles on key individuals, corporate foundations, and nonprofit organizations. In addition to publishing articles on laws, regulations, volunteerism, and fundraising, the publication reports on recent grants, conferences, seminars, events, and job openings. The *Chronicle of Philanthropy* also

> **Tip...**
>
> **Smart Tip**
> You can find at least some of the reference materials you need in a library. You can get help building your initial list of prospects by talking to library staff members, who can point you to the appropriate reference section and to specific newsletters, books, and directories.

provides classified advertisements for jobs in grant writing and fundraising. For more information or to subscribe, visit www.philanthropy.com.

LRP Publications

LRP Publications publishes five commercial newsletters: *Corporate Philanthropy Report*, *Education Grants Alert*, *Federal Grants and Contracts Weekly*, *Foundation and Corporate Grants Alert*, and *Health Grants & Contracts Weekly*. For more information go to www.lrp.com.

The *Grant Advisor*

Since 1983, the *Grant Advisor* has provided information on grant research and fellowship opportunities for U.S. institutions of higher education and their faculties. This online information service (www.grantadvisor.com) provides details on funders and requires a subscription.

Grantsalert

Grantsalert gives the latest listings of funders with complete web site information. After logging on to www.grantsalert.com, applicants can type in a category (i.e., colleges and universities; corporate; federal; fellowships; foundations; state), then select a field such as arts, writing, health, etc.

Subscription Databases

Subscription databases provide comprehensive, organized information on grant makers. Many databases allow you to search for key words, such as foundation name, state, city, fields of interest, types of support, geographic focus, trustees, officers, donors, and grant-maker types.

Guidestar

GuideStar provides information on the programs and finances of American charities and nonprofit organizations, articles about grant-making activities, up-to-date stories on philanthropy, and a forum for donors and volunteers. To learn more, visit www.guidestar.org.

Annual Reports

Annual reports and guidelines provide the detailed information that can help you decide if you should apply to a particular foundation. Most annual reports provide information on previously funded projects. Getting an idea of previously funded applicants may help you determine whether your project qualifies with the funding criteria of specific foundations.

The annual reports usually provide detailed information about a foundation's giving policies. They may summarize the foundation's history and why it was established, then outline the major kinds of programs and projects the company has funded. Annual reports also generally list the names of grant recipients, brief histories of their affiliations, and the amounts they received.

Some foundations mail out their annual reports upon request. You can also call the funder directly and request it, or sometimes, the Foundation Center may have it.

990-PF Reports

All foundations are required to file an annual "private foundation information return"—a 990-PF—with the Internal Revenue Service (IRS). The 990-PFs (www.form990.org) are the private foundation equivalents of Form 1040 income tax records of individuals. An organization's tax returns can be viewed online and also be made available upon a visit or a written request to the organization. These forms are becoming increasingly public and nonprofits are legally required to provide them to anyone wishing to see them.

The 990-PF must state the foundation's assets and how many grants were given each year. These information forms must be filed each year with the IRS by organizations that are exempt from federal income taxes (under Section 501 of the Internal Revenue Code) and have receipts of more than $25,000 a year. While there are many types of 501 organizations, those with 501(c)(3) status are exempt due to their charitable, educational, or religious purposes.

Smart Tip

Tip...

You can order foundation returns by contacting the Public Affairs Office at your local IRS headquarters. You will need to know the full name of the foundation, the city and state where it is located, and the year of the return you are ordering. To access 990-PF forms electronically, the Foundation Center has a link at www.fdncenter.org/funders/grantsmart/index.html or visit Guidestar at www.guidestar.org.

The 990-PF is an invaluable research tool, because it lists at least some examples of grants given during the year as well as actual recipients and amounts. Even more important, the 990-PF is a way to find out about small private foundations that might not appear in any directories or listings. Most importantly, the 990-PF allows grant seekers to access the source of the funder's assets and learn about recent grantees. This data may be more accurate than what is published on an organization's web site or in other publications.

Locating Grants by Field

As mentioned earlier, grants are awarded in a variety of fields, ranging from the arts to homeland security. Here are a few common categories of grants and places where you can find information about them.

Art Grants

Forget the starving artist. You can become a thriving artist if you know the right places to look for grants. Artists also qualify for various awards, scholarships, and research grants. Here are some places to look.

Fundsnet Services

Since 1996, Fundsnet Services has provided grant-writing and fundraising resource assistance. Fundsnet Services is an excellent, free source that lists thousands of funders. It is easy to access and is user-friendly. Fundsnet Services allows you to search for grant opportunities in various categories, including arts, children, disability, women, health, education, computers, technology, environment, sport, as well as computer and technology. Visitors can also link to pages on community foundations, international foundations, government funders, Canadian funders, and more. Learn more at www.fundsnetservices.com.

www.Mickeys-Place-in-the-Sun

This is an excellent resource for the beginner and advanced grant writer. This web site, www.mickeys-place-in-the-sun.com, is free and user-friendly. Its home page is divided into three sections:

1. community resources;
2. funding resources; and
3. additional resources.

The community resources section lists several categories of funding, including education, arts, health, and community development. The funding resources section lists thousands of listings of funders. The additional resources section contains other information about the field.

Council on Foundations

When you go to www.cof.org, you can link to government grants sources and private sector foundations. The Council on Foundations provides information on foundations awarding grants; upcoming events, such as grants conferences and career programs; how to start a foundation; grant-making activities; and fundraising publications.

Education Grants

Private foundations, federal funders, family trusts, community foundations, corporations, and individual families offer a wide variety of programs for funding higher education. Grants are awarded for individuals and organizations. Areas of funding include:

- College tuition
- International projects and travel
- Career advancement
- Research and professional support
- Cultural preservation
- Start-up costs for small businesses
- Emergency living expenses
- Medical and scientific research

The Fellowship and Assistantship Division's Foundation Hotlist

This site, www.grad.washington.edu/fellow/hotlist.htm, is useful for graduate students, scholars, and academic professionals. Information about grant funding for students and faculty is provided in detail here. The hot list also provides information on fellowships and assistantships. There is a separate section that lists funding resources for women and minorities.

College Scholarships, Graduate Fellowships, and Postdoctoral Awards for Minorities

This is an excellent site that gives hundreds of scholarships, awards, grants, college scholarships,

Smart Tip

The Foundation and Assistantship Division's Foundation Hot List (at www.grad.washington.edu/fellow/hotlist.htm) is highly recommended for those interested in obtaining funds for graduate school admissions, graduate school loans, travel research, awards, and fellowships.

graduate fellowships, and postdoctoral awards for minorities. Learn more at http://scholarships.fatomei.com/minorities.html.

Grantsnet

At Grantsnet, you can find funds for training in science and undergraduate science education. Grantsnet's service is free at www.grantsnet.org. From the Grantsnet site, you can also access the International Grants and Fellowship index.

Fastweb Student Services

This is a comprehensive resource for students seeking funding for college and graduates seeking job opportunities. The web site (www.studentservices.com/fastweb) is divided into three sections: scholarships; colleges (which includes profiles and scholarships); and jobs and internships (which lists career opportunities for graduates and students).

Stat Fact

Fastweb (www.student services.com/fastweb/lists) gives 1.3 million scholarships worth more than $3 billion.

The Financial Aid Page

This web site (www.finaid.org) lists scholarships and loans as well as financial aid applications and other information related to the financial aid process. You also can learn how to fill out financial aid forms. The Financial Aid Page also provides information on military aid, testing, college admissions, and jobs.

International Grants

Grants are awarded for various international education projects. Examples include academic research, disaster relief, archival preservation, teaching English as a second language, art exhibitions, environmental conservation, conferences, workshops, and humanitarian work. International grants are awarded to individuals and organizations.

Institute of International Education (IIE)

IIE, an independent nonprofit organization founded in 1919, is a world leader in the exchange of people and ideas, administering more than 200 programs that serve more than 20,000 individuals each year. The institute's web site (www.iie.org) lists more than 7,000 opportunities to combine travel and study worldwide under "Research and Resources."

Smart Tip

Tip...

The Institute of International Education (www.iie.org) provides information on the Fulbright scholarship program.

The Global Fund for Women

The Global Fund for Women supports women's groups that advance the human rights of women and girls. It strengthens women's-rights groups based outside the United States by providing small, flexible, and timely grants ranging from $500 to $20,000 for operating and program expenses. Learn more at www.globalfundfor women.org. See the image below for the types of grants issued by this organization.

Ashoka Foundation

Ashoka (www.ashoka.org) envisions a world where everyone is a changemaker: a world that responds quickly and effectively to social challenges, and where each individual has the freedom, confidence, and societal support to address any social problem and drive change.

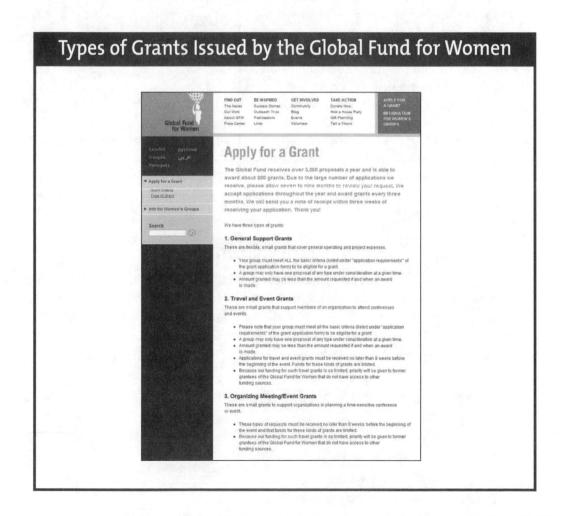

Types of Grants Issued by the Global Fund for Women

Ashoka strives to shape a global, entrepreneurial, competitive citizen sector: one that allows social entrepreneurs to thrive and enables the world's citizens to think and act as changemakers.

Asian Cultural Council

The Asian Cultural Council (www.asianculturalcouncil.org/) is a foundation supporting cultural exchange in the visual and performing arts between the United States and Asia. Grants are made in the following fields: archaeology, architecture (design, theory, and history), art history, art and architectural conservation, crafts, dance, film, musicology, music, painting, photography, printmaking, sculpture, theater, and video.

Studyabroad.com

Studyabroad.com (www.studyabroad.com) is the internet's leading source of information on educational opportunities for students to study in other countries. It is a comprehensive directory of study abroad programs, including summer study abroad, internship, service learning and volunteer abroad programs, intensive language programs and more, all organized by subject or country or city. International education support through their study abroad handbook provides a guide to education abroad: health, safety, and study abroad scholarship/financial aid information.

> **Tip...**
>
> **Smart Tip**
> Studyabroad.com offers information on academic programs overseas; summer programs in Europe, Asia, Australia, Africa, and Latin America; programs organized by city; and information on thousands of language programs.

Emergency Grants

The loss of a job, hospital bills, the death of a family member, and natural disasters are all examples of sudden and unforeseen circumstances that can throw one's financial stability out of control. In the world of grants, these are known as "emergency" or "general welfare" expenses.

Supporting documents generally required for emergency grant applications include:

- Copies of bills for which assistance is being requested
- Your resume
- Your most recent bank statement
- Your most recent tax return
- Your mortgage/rent payment
- References who can testify on your behalf

Mayer Foundation

The Mayer Foundation has grants of up to $5,000 available to individuals who find themselves in severe economic turmoil due to natural or civil disasters. Grants are awarded to cover rent, mortgage, medical bills, utilities, and other day-to-day living expenses. See www.mayerfoundation.org for details.

> **Tip...**
>
> **Smart Tip**
>
> Emergency grants are usually awarded to individuals without institutional affiliation. Emergency grants are based on need, and given to pay for rent, medical bills, utilities, detoxification, drug rehabilitation, and food.

National Association for the Self-Employed

This membership organization provides access to health insurance for the self-employed. See www.nase.org/nase_benefits/membership_levels.asp for details.

Change, Inc.

Grants of up to $1,000 are available to artists for medical, living, and other expenses. For an application, write to PO Box 705, Cooper Station, New York, NY 10276 or call (212) 226-0581.

Author's League Fund

The Author's League Fund offers interest-free loans of between $2,000 and $3,000 to writers with severe medical or health-related problems and other serious misfortunes. No membership is necessary. Application and details available at www.authorsleaguefund.org.

Writer's Guild of America

Health insurance available for members. To become a member, applicants must meet extensive eligibility requirements, found at www.wga.org.

> **Stat Fact**
>
> The Foundation Center survey conducted in March, 2007, records Tulsa Community Foundation in Oklahoma as the largest community foundation by asset size, with assets totaling $2,264,564,027 by the fiscal year end date December 31, 2005.

PEN Writer's Fund

Grants of up to $2,000 are available to published writers in "acute, financial crisis." No membership is necessary to apply for emergency assistance. Application and details are available at www.pen.org. The figure on page 46 shows sample guidelines for the PEN Writer's Fund emergency grants, given to individuals to cover living expenses, such as rent, medical bills, and debt payment.

PEN Writer's Fund Grant Information

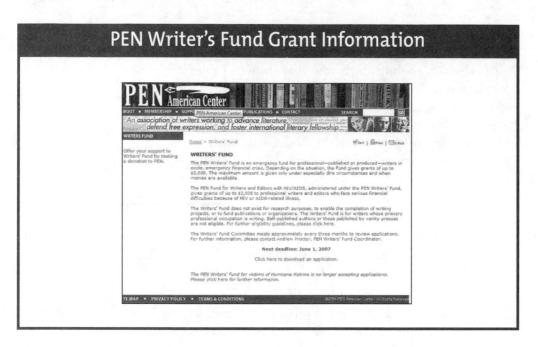

Actor's Fund Financial Assistance Programs

Several emergency aid programs are available—with specific eligibility requirements—to applicants with five years' experience working in entertainment who have
earned a minimum of $6,500 per year in the industry. See www.actorsfund.org for
details.

Poets In Need

Emergency assistance is available to poets who have an established presence in the
literary community as innovators in the field and have a substantive body of published
work. For information, see www.poetsinneed.org.

Understanding
the Funders'
Guidelines

With any funder, remember to read the application guidelines carefully before writing your proposal. Simple as it may sound, this advice is very important. Because funders receive so many applications, those that do not strictly comply with the funder's instructions are often quickly discarded. You may have excellent grant-proposal writing skills and an uncanny ability to submit winning proposals, but if you don't know how to read the guidelines and follow them, the likelihood of submitting a successful proposal is slim.

Ten years ago, hard copies of directories were the standard method of hunting for grants. They are still widely used, but the internet is gaining more popularity when it comes to researching funders. In addition, the internet often has more up-to-date information than hard-bound directories, which are only published once a year.

> **Smart Tip** Tip...
>
> Targeting your applications to the right sources is key. Submit applications to the funder who has an interest in the type of work you do, who has the money to give away, and whose mission statement agrees with your philosophy.

What Grant Writers Need to Gather from the Guidelines

When you read about a funder either online or in a directory, look for the following information:

- *Eligibility.* This section lays out any eligibility requirements, such as if grants are awarded only to organizations or individuals.

- *Foundation's purpose.* Check to make sure the funder shares an interest in your project or targets the same population as your project. Also check for geographic priorities. If the foundation makes only local grants and your organization is on the other side of the state, cross that particular foundation off your list. Conversely, if the foundation makes national grants, ensure your project has national importance before submitting an application.

- *Funding amount.* Here you can get an indication of the size of the grants the funder typically awards. Some funders even give a range, such as "between $10,000 and $500,000." Note that this information is published in directories (see Chapter 4) but rarely in guidelines received directly from a foundation.

- *Areas of funding.* This section lists fields that the foundation prefers to fund.

- *Restrictions.* Most foundations also provide a paragraph on what they will not fund. Examples of restrictions may include operating support, program-related investments/loans, endorsements, publications, conferences/seminars, special events/sponsorships, grants to individuals, scholarships, fellowships, educational loans, travel grants, research grants, or religious-based projects.

- *Limitations.* You may find statements of limitations such as "Grant funds are generally limited to charitable organizations already favorably known to the foundation" or "Grant funds are committed." Both statements mean the same thing: the foundation already is working with established organizations and has committed money to those same organizations year

Beware!
Some foundations have two addresses: a physical address and an application address. Be sure to send your application to the proper address.

after year. Another statement you might see is "No unsolicited proposals considered," which means you should submit an application only after you have met with a foundation representative who is willing to learn more about your project.

- *Deadline.* Be sure you know when your application must be submitted by.
- *Contact information.* This section typically describes how to obtain an application form and how to submit a completed application.

Sample Guidelines

Guidelines vary from funder to funder. Here are three sample guidelines:

Sample Guidelines from a Private Foundation

To apply to the foundation, please submit a three-page application. Applications over three pages will not be considered. Electronic submissions in Microsoft Word® or PDF formats are also accepted. On the first two pages include the following:

1. Title of the project
2. A brief (two sentence) description of the project
3. Overall objective and significance of and benefit from your project
4. Clearly and in detail set forth the specific goals of your project, how you will accomplish these goals, and the time frame for the project. The foundation will primarily focus on stated goals and the plan to accomplish them in reviewing all requests
5. On a separate single page please provide:
   a. The dollar amount requested and the specific budget for the project and its justification. The foundation generally does not provide funds for organization overhead, routine equipment, standard photographic equipment or personal computers. Any related funding, active or pending, including "in-kind" funds should be explicitly described, including the budget.

b. The applicant's name, address, and phone number

c. Any affiliations of the applicant

d. Identify all previous requests to the foundation

All applications must be mailed (postmarked) no later than June 30th, 2006. Successful applicants will be notified by December 30th, 2006. Funds will be disbursed shortly thereafter. Use regular mail. Do not use a mail service that requires staff signature.

Sample Guidelines from a Federal Funder

Here are more complex guidelines by a federal funder.

1. *Application cover sheet.* Complete the application cover sheet given online and attach a copy to the application. Project title should be brief, descriptive, and substantive.

2. *Statement of significance and impact.* Provide a one-page abstract written for a non-specialist audience stating clearly the importance of the proposed work and its relation to larger issues in the arts and humanities.

3. *Table of contents.* List all parts of the application and corresponding page numbers.

4. *List of participants.* On a separate page list in alphabetical order, surnames first, all project participants and collaborators and their institutional affiliations, if any. This list will be used to ensure that prospective panelists and reviewers have no conflict of interest with the project that they will be evaluating. This list should include advisory board members, if any.

5. *Narrative description.* Applicants should provide an intellectual justification for the project and a work plan. Narrative descriptions are limited to forty double-spaced pages. All pages should have one-inch margins and the font size should be no smaller than 11 points. Use appendices to provide supplementary materials. Applicants should keep in mind the criteria used to evaluate proposals. Provide a detailed description consisting of the following sections:

   a. *Substance and context.* Provide a clear and concise explanation of the project and its value to scholars, students, and general audiences in the arts. Describe the scope of the research, source materials, the relationships of the research to other published and ongoing work in the field, and major issues to be addressed. Include a bibliographical essay in the narrative section or a bibliography of relevant primary and secondary sources in an appendix.

   b. *History and duration of project.* Provide a concise history of the project, including information about preliminary research or planning, previous financial support, publications produced, and resources or research facilities available. List any volumes, microform products, or electronic products produced with dates of publication; where applicable, the list should indicate the publisher, print or production runs, sales and royalties. Provide reviews of the most recent volume or other product in an appendix. If an archaeological excavation is proposed, list publications of previous field reports and interpretive studies of the site. If the project has a web site, provide its address.

c. *Staff.* Identify the project director and collaborators, describing their responsibilities and qualifications. Provide resumes for the principal collaborators in an appendix. Project directors must devote a significant portion of their time to their projects. If the project has an advisory board, provide a statement of its function and a list of board members.

d. *Methods.* Explain how central research questions will be approached and how any potential difficulties in working with primary source materials will be resolved. Describe in detail the tasks to be undertaken and the computer technology to be employed, indicating what technical and staff resources will be required, as well as the staff's experience with the technology and its application to humanities scholarship. Applicants proposing fieldwork should discuss the appropriateness of the methodology, including a clear, explicit discussion of the links between the project's interpretive questions, the data, and the methods of collection and analysis.

e. *Final product and dissemination.* Describe publication plans and provide, if possible, an outline of the publication. Include in an appendix any pertinent correspondence with a publisher such as a letter of interest. Applicants should discuss the form chosen for the final product (printed articles or books, microform, electronic media, or some combination) and the rationale for the choice. If the project involves materials under copyright, the applicant should indicate what has been done to secure the necessary permission to publish.

f. *Work plan.* Describe what will be accomplished during each six-month period and identify the staff members involved. The work described in the proposal should be completed by the end of the grant period.

6. *Project budget.* Use the attached budget sheet for a detailed cost computation of project income and expenses.

7. *Appendices.* Use appendices to provide essential supplementary materials. All appendices should not total more than 35 pages. Include a brief resume for each principal project participant and letters of commitment from other participants and cooperating institutions. Assessments of previous applications and testimonials should not be included. Include a bibliography of relevant primary and secondary literature in an appendix.

For archaeological excavations include appropriate plans, maps, and photographs, as well as evidence that all necessary permits will be forthcoming.

For translations provide five-to-seven pages, double-spaced sample of the translation to be undertaken with appropriate sample annotations and a photocopy of the same passage in the original language. Choose passages that show the importance and the degree of difficulty of the text.

8. *List of suggested evaluators.* On a separate sheet of paper, provide the names, full mailing addresses, and e-mail addresses of six to eight persons who can provide impartial evaluations of the proposal. Explain briefly each person's qualifications as an evaluator. Do not, however, discuss the proposal with the potential evaluators. Previous applicants should revise the list of suggested evaluators to include several persons not named in the earlier application. The evaluators should be scholars whose expertise and broad knowledge lend weight to their judgments.

Deadlines for Submission

Applications must be received by December 30th, 2008, 5 P.M.

Sample Guidelines for an Online Application

Please list full name of the foundation to which you are applying: _____

_____

General Information

Organization name: _____

Address: _____

City/state/zip: _____

Phone: _____ Fax: _____

E-mail: _____ Web site: _____

Contact person/position: _____ Contact phone: _____

Grant Request

Date of request: _____

Amount requested: $ _____

Sample Guidelines for an Online Application, continued

Total project cost: $ _____

Total organization budget for this year: $ _____

Statement of Organization's Mission or Purpose: _____

_____

_____

_____

Names and Roles of Organization's Key Leadership (Staff): _____

1. _____

2. _____

3. _____

Project or Purpose of Grant Request: _____

_____

_____

_____

Impact of Grant Requested on your Organization and the Community: ____

_____

_____

_____

Evaluation

Briefly explain: _____

_____

_____

_____

Sample Guidelines for an Online Application, continued

The Timetable for Specific Goals and Objectives:

_____

_____

_____

6

The Grant
Proposal

Now you are ready to start writing. Be sure to take some time and go through all the stages—from initial draft to final submission. A grant proposal should never be rushed. Be sure to allow yourself time to reflect on what has been written, as the perspective you gain from letting the proposal sit for a bit is worthwhile. All these elements are explored further in this chapter.

The grant proposal is the main link connecting a grant writer with a funder. It is essentially, a document of persuasion. Funders are persuaded in simple language, why they should invest their philanthropic dollars in specific requests.

The Four Stages of Crafting a Persuasive Grant Proposal

Very few grant proposals are written in one sitting. They have to undergo extensive rewriting before the final submission takes place. Here are the four stages of crafting a persuasive grant proposal:

1. *The initial draft.* The initial draft sets the tone and direction as well as provides the framework for your proposal. The ensuing drafts are based on the first draft. It is recommended that the initial draft be written when your mind is fresh and alert.

2. *Editing.* The strongest grant proposals are those that have undergone extensive revision. Editing helps detect typos, inconsistencies, redundancies, and grammatical errors. Some grant writers are better at editing using several short periods of time while others are better at editing a proposal for several hours at a stretch.

> **Tip...**
>
> **Smart Tip**
> After you complete an initial draft, let your grant proposal "marinate" for a couple of days. This helps you to look at it from a fresh perspective.

3. *The "marinating" stage.* After you have edited the proposal a few times, allow it to sit for a week or so. Focus your mind on other things besides the application you just completed. This marinating stage does wonders to help you see the proposal from a fresh perspective.

4. *Submission.* Once the proposal is edited and revised, compile all supporting documentation required and submit the package according to the grant instructions.

Time Required to Create a Grant Proposal

How much time to spend on a grant proposal depends in part, on the deadline, application's level of difficulty, length, and supporting materials. Typically, grant writers spend between one week and four months on a single grant proposal. (A proposal's length requirements vary, ranging from 3 to 50 pages or more. A technical and research-oriented proposal may be even longer.) Regardless of length and order, proposal basics are the same, and the information included in each section is integral to any successful funding request.

The length of time required to create a proposal also depends on the type of grant application and the grant writer's level of expertise on the topic. As a general rule, an experienced grant writer's hourly estimate for a project is within the ranges listed below. These estimates include meetings with clients, filling out forms, writing budgets, writing the grant proposal, and revising. Minor time expenses—such as those for shipping, mailing, or running to the courier service—are not included.

Project	Time Required (in hours)
Federal grants	40 to 60
Specialized grants	100 to 180
Foundation grants	3 to 8
Corporate-giving program grants	3 to 8
State/local government grants	10 to 20
Foundation grant for individuals	2 to 8

You will find it takes longer to write your first few grants. It also is likely to take more time when you write a grant for a new client. But as you work with clients on subsequent proposals, you accumulate "canned" text that you can use over and over again. For instance, several paragraphs in your statement of need must describe the organization and those it serves.

Once a client approves your text and you have a successful grant proposal for the client, there is no need to reinvent the wheel. Recycling the information saves time. This information is then called "boilerplate."

The Elements of a Grant Proposal

Regardless of the funder, the basics of a grant proposal are the same, and the information included in each section is integral to any successful funding request. The order of the proposal components may vary, depending on the funding organization and the type of grant you seek. The main components of a grant proposal are:

- Cover letter
- Abstract
- Table of contents (TOC)
- Need statement
- Goals and objectives
- Methodology

▲

Grant Awards

According to the Foundation Center, the median grant award is $25,000. The following represents the breakdown of grant distribution by size as reported by foundation giving trends.

○ 38.6 percent between $10,000 and $24,999

○ 23.2 percent between $25,000 and $49,000

○ 16 percent between $50,000 and 99,999

○ 17.8 percent between $100,000 and $499,999

○ 0.1 percent above $10 million

- Budget
- Evaluation and dissemination

Cover Letter

The cover letter is the first piece in your proposal package, and serves as the formal introduction for your organization and proposal. The type of information to be included in the cover letter depends on the grant narrative, the amount of funding requested, and the length of the proposal. The cover letter ideally should be one to two pages long.

Some funders ask applicants to fill out a provided cover letter (sometimes called an application sheet). When one is provided, you should not write another cover letter of your own.

Tips for Writing the Cover Letter

Being aware of the following can help you write eye-grabbing cover letters.

- *Write short, pertinent, and substantial sentences.* Long sentences mean you are getting too narrative, and this is not recommended. Stay to the point. Don't digress and get into too much detail in your initial introduction. You cover letter needs to give substance to your project. Don't be shallow, cute, or too personal.

- *Highlight the key points that are discussed in more detail in the proposal.* In essence, the cover letter is a précis of your narrative, summing up the key points, and inviting the funder to make an investment in your project.

- *Submit a clear and readable letter.* Make your cover letter easy and simple. Don't be arrogant and demand money with sentences such as: "It is in your best interest to award our organization this grant. No one else can conduct this project as best as we can." This type of language does not impress funders.

Smart Tip
Write the cover letter last, i.e., after the proposal has been completed.

- *Address the letter to a specific individual—not "The Grants Officer" or "To whom it may concern."* Generally, the individual contact information is listed on the funder's web site. Be sure to correctly spell the person's name. If you do not have a contact person, call or e-mail the foundation and find out who is in charge of the grants program. Address the person by the last name with the proper salutation. For example, if the contact person's name is Dave Rodell, address him as "Mr./ Dr. Rodell," instead of "Dave."

- *Sign at the bottom.* If you are sending a hard-copy application, always remember to sign the cover letter. If you have completed a 50-page grant application and mail it out without signing the cover page, it may be disqualified. This is especially applicable with federal funders.

Sample Cover Letters

Take a look at the sample application sheet provided by a federal funder and the sample cover letter that has been individually crafted to a funder on pages 60 and 61, respectively.

The Abstract

An abstract is also called a summary, program summary, or executive summary. It is often the first thing a reader sees and may be your most important marketing tool. Usually the abstract is written last. The abstract summarizes and defines your project on a single page or sometimes in 300 words or so.

Keep your abstract basic. For example:

> Good Samaritan Shelter requests $5,000 for a two-year, $50,000 job training program for homeless women in Georgia. Training will be offered at four rural shelters and will include basic clerical skills, interview techniques, and job-seeker support groups.

The abstract usually contains the following elements:
- Identification of the applicant
- The applicant's qualifications to carry out the project

Application Sheet Provided by a Federal Funder

Application Cover Sheet

Research Grants

Individual Applicant

Full name: _____

Mailing address: _____

Phone (W): _____

Phone (H): _____

Fax: _____

Field of expertise: _____

Citizenship: _____

Institution: _____

Application information

Project title: _____

Grant period: _____

Sample Cover Letter Crafted to a Funder

May 15th, 20xx

Foundation Name
Street Address
City, State, Zip

Dear Ms. Ippstein,

I would like to apply for a grant from The Meyer Foundation. I am an individual applicant, seeking assistance to publish a book.

I am a food writer and have had hundreds of articles published in American, European, and Asian magazines. I am also the author of the book *Start Your Own Food Business*, published by Health Food, New York. As the editor of the *2007 Organic Food Directory*, I write, review, and edit food and spa articles for the Organic Food Association in California.

I would like to self-publish the book titled *Healing Foods*. I need financial support to pay copyediting fees, production and layout costs, and marketing-related expenses. The total amount that I need to publish the book is $3,500.

Thank you.

Sincerely yours,

Sheila Branson

Sheila Branson

▲

- The specific purpose of the grant
- The anticipated end result
- The amount of money requested
- The total project budget

Tips for Writing the Abstract

Here are six tips for writing the abstract.

1. *Decide what the key points are in each section of the proposal.* Include the key points in the summary. Stress the points that you know are important to the funder.

2. *Start with an arresting sentence.* Remember this is the first sentence your reviewer is likely going to read. Make your opening sentence interesting and colorful; avoid one that is negative.

3. *Establish credibility.* In brief, tell the funder about your organization and why it can be trusted to use funds effectively and honestly. The funder needs to be assured that philanthropic dollars will be used wisely.

4. *Write short sentences.* Eliminate wordiness in the abstract. It needs to be brief; the sentences, precise. You have to convince the funder about your project in a short word count. This is not the place to be writing a novel.

5. *Show the immediacy of the problem.* Give some statistics or paint an effective visual picture of the need to address the issue you have identified. Indicate how your project is going to make a positive difference in society.

6. *Stay within the word count specified in the guidelines.* You need to conform by the rules set forth by the funder. Don't think the funder is going to be impressed if you write a long abstract describing how wonderful your project is. If the funder asks for a 100-word abstract, for example, stick to it. You can get eliminated early in the application process if you don't.

Sample Abstract

Take a look at the sample 70-word abstract on page 63. It was submitted by an individual applicant who sought funds to conduct a photographic documentary:

Table of Contents

An optional element in a grant proposal, a table of contents (TOC), is typically used when your grant proposal is five or more pages. A TOC makes it easier on the reviewer for two main reasons. First, a TOC clearly shows you have included all the information the funder requested. Second, a TOC acts as a map of a complex document.

Sample Abstract

Abstract

Building Bridges: A Photographic Documentary on Inter-Cultural Relationships across America

Intercultural relationships are becoming a sign of our times. With globalization and ease of airplane travel, there have been large-scale migration patterns leading to cross cultural marriages. Building Bridges across America will be a photographic exhibition covering inter-cultural marriages across America. The purpose of my project is to promote understanding between different cultures. Through photography I want to create awareness and enhance our understanding of the similarities between people of different cultures.

Tips for Writing a Table of Contents

A TOC is fairly straightforward. But be sure to:

- *Include the TOC at the beginning of the proposal package.* If you are including a TOC it should be introduced right at the onset of the proposal. This will give the reviewer an indication of the elements that have been fleshed out within the proposal and where to find them.
- *Use page numbers.* A TOC is difficult to use if the pages are not numbered. Most computers have page number insertions. The common format is to insert the page numbers on the lower right side of the page.
- *Make sure the page numbers correspond to the headings.* Once the proposal has been written, double check that the page numbers and the section titles match.
- *Include the TOC on a page by itself.* Don't include any other information—such as contact information, the cover letter, or the abstract—on the TOC page. Devote a fresh page to the TOC.

Sample Table of Contents

Not all TOC will have the elements shown in the sample on page 64; some may have fewer headings. Choose the headings you need according to the guidelines established by the funder.

Smart Tip

A TOC in longer proposals is like a road map for your grant proposal.

Tip...

Sample Table of Contents

Table of Contents

Problem or Need Statement

The need statement clearly defines the project for which funds are being requested. The need statement is also known as the problem statement or situation description. It performs three purposes: It tells the funder the need for the project, the problem at hand, as well as the urgency and significance of the project.

At the heart of your case for financial support, the need statement indicates why the particular need or project should be of interest to the funder. It establishes that the applicant understands the problems and therefore can reasonably address them. The need statement studies the following questions: "Why is the project necessary? What is the issue? Why should we care?" In writing the need statement, do not assume everyone sees the problem as clearly as you do.

Need statements aim to assure the carefully targeted reader that the proposed project is the place to wisely invest philanthropic dollars. When identifying a problem, you must convince the funding source that the issue(s) you want to address are important to the advancement of both your and the funder's organizations.

Tips for Writing the Need Statement

Here are some guidelines for writing effective need statements. They are not hard-and-fast rules, but suggestions that can get your project a step closer to funding.

- *Don't describe the problem as the absence of your project.* You need to show that your project addresses the root cause of the situation and not just a superficial approach. "We don't have enough beds in our battered women's shelter" is not the problem. The problem is increased levels of domestic violence. A solution is to tighten the laws against physical and emotional violence.

- *Relate your problem to the interests and priorities of the funder.* Explain the consequences and results of the issues and needs that are being discussed within the proposal. Define the local or national problem to be addressed and why you are qualified to address it.

- *Provide some perspective.* Acknowledge other individuals or organizations working in your field. You don't want the funding source to think that you are unaware of other projects or that your project is a duplication and therefore unnecessary. Show how your project is different and what unmet needs your project will address. Connect with others; don't isolate your project as superior.

- *Describe the target population to be served.* Describe your population and its issues/needs. Explain why you have chosen this specific target population. If possible, cite specific cases of interest in the proposal. Including testimonials also adds credibility to your need statement.

- *Quantify your need.* Provide facts or statistics supporting your project. Unsupported assumptions do not create a compelling case for your specific needs. Ground your need statement in fact, not opinion. Information that is too generic or broad does not help you develop a winning argument for your project.

- *Weigh the gravity of the problem.* Determine whether it is reasonable to portray the need as acute. Every need statement does not have to pose a life-threatening situation. What is important, however, is convincing the funder that the problem you are addressing requires attention or that the solution you are proposing offers hope for improvement.

- *The problem to be addressed should have a clear relationship to your mission and purpose.* The problem that is described in the proposal should be consistent with your scope to respond to that problem. You must prove you have the qualifications and skills to complete the project successfully.

Smart Tip

Leave hope in your need statement. The picture you paint should not be so grim that the situation appears hopeless. The funder will wonder whether an investment in your project is worthwhile. Show that there is room for positive change to occur.

Sample Need Statement

Here is a sample need statement submitted by an individual applicant:

Sample Needs Statement

Roads to Sobriety

"Roads to Sobriety" will be a research project examining the crippling effects caused by alcoholism among families in Sri Lanka. Alcoholism is a major problem in Sri Lanka. One of every three families has an active male alcoholic whose drinking interferes with family peace and obstructs community development.

The Foundation for Mental Health wants to study the issue of alcoholism and how it can be addressed at the grassroots level. During previous studies conducted by a team of medical professionals and social service workers, it was concluded that the majority of health professionals are misinformed about alcoholism. They encourage alcoholics in the fallacy of controlled drinking. Topics addressed in the study will include alcohol treatment, prevention, and education.

As part of the proposed project, the Foundation for Mental Health hopes to initiate an alcohol rehabilitation center in Sri Lanka. It will provide hope for thousands of families crippled by a loved one's drinking and show that life can be enjoyed without the bottle.

Source: The Foundation for Mental Health, Sri Lanka, is a NGO specializing in the mental health field. Statistics were taken from the Ministry of Health, Sri Lanka.

Goals and Objectives

The goals and objectives section defines the solution proposed to address the problem described in the need statement. The goals and objectives are the anticipated outcomes of the planned program. They offer a clear picture of the results of implementing your program and identify how the problem(s) will be addressed. This section is usually written after the need statement and addresses the following question: what would this situation look like if it were changed?

Defining Goals

Goals, also referred to as *work-plan specific activities*, represent the project's ideal, long-range benefits. Goals are where you want to be when the funds are used up; they are broad-based statements of the ultimate result of the change being undertaken, a result that is sometimes unreachable in the short term. Grant application narratives must have goals to show the funder that you have a "big picture" vision for solving the problem. The goal describes the general impact you hope to have on the problem you have defined, without necessarily indicating the magnitude.

Goals are usually presented in terms of hopes, wishes, or desires. Typical goal-oriented words include "appreciate," "understand," "advocate," "analyze," "illustrate," "participate," "integrate," and "recommend."

Tips for Writing Goals

- *Identify project goals that are within your or your organization's competence and expertise.* The goals must fit the mission and scope of your organization. Here is a general example of a goal: "Sober Living—a nonprofit organization that identifies with the high rate of alcoholism among retired senior citizens in Madison County—aims to reduce the numbers of senior citizens separating themselves from society and confining themselves to the bottle." Another example of a goal is: "Rose Foundation is a small, nonprofit organization that will create jobs for unemployed youth in Garfield County." Despite the vague nature of the goals cited above, they are realistic for a community agency to achieve. An unrealistic goal for a small nonprofit in Madison County would be to reduce alcoholism among senior citizens throughout the United States or for the Rose Foundation to create jobs for unemployed youth throughout the United States.

- *Do not specify the magnitude of the reduction, the time frame for achieving the goal, or the effects of reaching the goal.* Simply explain what your organization plans to do about the problem. You might say: "The goals of this project are to increase the understanding among Colorado middle school students about the impact of smoking on their health, and to reduce the number of students who smoke."

- Provide concrete examples showing previous experiences in this field or in related areas. This gives an indication of your capacity to carry out the proposed project.
- Describe the population that will benefit from your project. Give details, including how you will involve the target audience in the activity and how many people you intend to serve. Some projects have two audiences: the *direct participants* (e.g., the musicians in the community band or the kids doing summer cleanup in the parks) and the *indirect beneficiaries* (e.g., the music lovers in the audience or the people who use the parks). If so, describe both. How will you ensure people participate in the program?

> **Tip...**
>
> **Smart Tip**
>
> Demonstrate that your goals are important, significant, and timely. Choose goals that are strategic. For example, for a U.S.-based organization, a topic on cyber-terrorism is current, whereas education rights for women is past.

Defining Objectives

Objectives—also known as *outcomes* or *impact of activities*—are steps that lead up to the goals. An objective is a major milestone or checkpoint on your route to a goal, and is much more narrowly defined than a goal. Like goals, objectives are tied to the need statement. Objectives have to be attainable and serve to keep goals realistic.

Your objective section is the intellectual heart of the proposal, because it is where you indicate precisely what you intend to change through your project and what you will accept as proof of your project's success. Use action words in the infinitive form such as "to analyze," "to advocate," "to anticipate," "to decrease," "to increase," "to motivate," "to categorize," "to construct," "to design," and "to illustrate." When sponsors fund your project they are literary "buying" your objectives.

Types of Objectives

The two main types of objectives are
1. process, or implementation, objectives, and
2. outcome objectives.

Process objectives refer to a series of actions directed toward a particular aim. You discuss what you plan to do in the process objectives. You can tell if you have written a process objective if you started with words such as "to provide," "to develop," or "to establish." A process objective is abstract in its wording.

> **Tip...**
>
> **Smart Tip**
>
> Objectives are specific, measurable activities that will help to achieve the goals.

Outcome objectives state a quantifiable result of the project and deal with program impact. Look for words such as "to increase" or "to decrease"; they imply some sort of measurable change.

Tips for Writing Objectives

- State objectives in terms of outcomes. Give numbers when possible and create a concrete picture of what the situation will look like once you address the need at hand. The objective section shows that you can produce definite outcomes. Include objectives that comprehensively describe the intended outcomes of the project.

- Demonstrate that your objectives stem directly from the statement of need. For example, if there is a need to address the use of illegal drugs among teens, your objective should be to reduce the growing use of drugs in your community.

- State when the objectives are scheduled to be accomplished. Give an exact date as to when the project is going to take place. If you are submitting a proposal with phases, list your specific objectives in expected chronological order of achievement.

- Like goals, objectives should clearly identify the population being served. For example, if your project focuses on drug use among youth, identify the age groups: 12–18, 18–25, etc. Also state if you are targeting specific races.

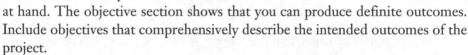

Beware!

Avoid confusing your objectives (ends) with your methods (means). A good objective emphasizes what will be done and when it will be done, whereas a method explains how it will be done.

Smart Tip

The methodology section is also known as a statement of work, activities, approach, strategies, or procedures. Methods are closely linked to the goals and objectives of a proposal. The objectives tell reviewers what you propose to do, whereas the methods section tells how you are going to achieve the objectives.

Sample Goals and Objectives

Take a look at the example of goals and objectives on page 70 submitted by an environmental organization wanting to research the feeding patterns of leopards in Yala National Park, Sri Lanka.

Methodology

The methodology section of a grant proposal tells who is going to do what and when it will be done. It addresses the following question: "What can the organization or individual do to change the existing situation?" The methods are the action plans that allow the

Sample Goals and Objectives

Goals and Objectives

Researching the Feeding Ecology and Reproductive Behavioral Patterns of Leopards

Goal #1: To study the feeding patterns of leopards in Yala National Park, Sri Lanka

The aims are to gather accurate information about what leopards eat. I will study the scat of leopards in order to get an idea of their feeding patterns. The objectives will address the following:

1. Are hair fragments, skin fragments, fish scales and bird feathers found?

2. If so, what types of animals do they belong to?

3. What are the main forms of prey found in the scat?

Goal #2: To study the reproductive behavioral patterns of leopards in Yala National Park, Sri Lanka

The aims are to find out about the reproductive patterns of leopards. Knowing the seasons, weather conditions, and population factors affecting the reproductive behaviors of leopards can help in getting better results in learning about the breeding of leopards. The objectives will address the following:

1. Is there a higher frequency of mating during a certain time of the year? For example, is there a higher frequency of mating during the rainy season than during the dry season?

2. What is the gestation period of leopards?

3. Till what age do cubs follow their mothers?

4. How many litter do leopards typically give birth to? Do all the cubs survive?

5. What is the average life span of leopards?

organization to reach the goals and objectives discussed in the proposal. Typically, each objective is accompanied by one or more methods.

The methods prove to the reviewer that your organization has the qualifications, credibility, and capacity to carry out the proposed project efficiently. The methodology section usually requires a fairly detailed account of the activities that will take place during the project.

The methodology section of a grant proposal addresses three basic components:

1. *How.* This is a detailed description of what will occur from the time the project begins until it is completed.

2. *When.* This is the order and timing for the project tasks to take place.

3. *Why.* In some cases, you may need to defend your chosen methods, especially if they are new or unorthodox.

Tips for Writing the Methodology

Paying attention to the following can help you to polish your methodology section:

- *Explain why you chose a specific methodological approach.* Each project requires a specific kind of method. For example, the methods used by an actor for a broadway musical by Kurt Weill may be different from what a surgeon would use for a groundbreaking brain surgery.

   Some methods used by artists include still photography, videotapes, publications, digital photography, musical recordings, face-to-face interviews, and photographic archives.

   Whereas common methods that social scientists and medical practitioners employ include survey research; formal, intensive interviewing; participant observation; library research; archival research; experiments on animals (only within limits and under specific animal-rights guidelines); and aerial photography.

- *Describe the major activities for reaching each objective.* Describe what you are going to do. Tell the funder about the project's "outcome." Be sure your proposal doesn't promise an unrealistic level of service. Unrealistic objectivities can go against your proposal.

- *Indicate the key project personnel who will carry out each activity.* List who is going to do the work and their credentials. You may even attach current resumes of key people. Some funders ask for the name of a project director, the person most responsible for the project. If there is more than one person organizing the event, give all their names.

- *Show the interrelationships among project activities.* Show a clear connection between the people participating in the project and their level of involvement. Some of the participants may benefit directly as a result of the project methodology, while others may benefit from behind the scenes. Describe all population groups who are likely to get something out of it. Include a time and task chart, such as the one in the sample methodology below.

- *Include a time and task chart.* This is also known as the work plan and tells when the project will take place. Some funders will ask for the project start date and project end date. If the project is long, i.e., over a year, consider including a timeline of the different phases. In simple terms, this gives the funder a clear picture of the steps you will take to accomplish each objective identified in the goals and objectives section.

Sample Methodology

EcoAsia nonprofit organization that applied for funding to develop an eco-friendly fishing net to trap crabs in Sri Lanka. Instead of describing the crab classification system in a paragraph, and overwhelming the funder with wordiness, the grant writer conveyed the system with a diagram as in the sample.

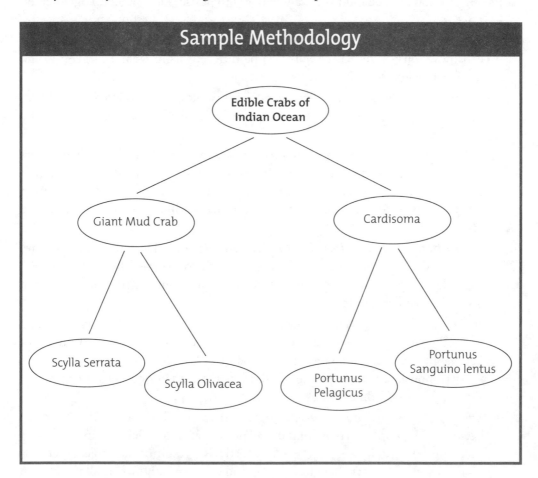

Sample Methodology

Methodology

Crab Fishing and Marine Conservation

This was part of the methodology submitted by the RPK Foundation, Sri Lanka.

Prior to departing to the field, my principal research assistant and I will prepare a sample questionnaire to interview 100 fishermen engaged in crab fishing. Our principal guide will be McAllester's suggestions for conducting face-to-face interviews in the field. I will ask the questions and my assistant will record them through a portable mini cassette player. At the end of the day we will transcribe the interviews and enter them into the computer in the Microsoft Word® program.

The choice of questions will target crab fishing methods, risks involved, and the kinds of shell fish caught in nets. Some sample questions include:

1. About how many crabs do you catch per day?

2. What types of crabs do you catch the most? How can you distinguish one from the other?

3. Do you sell all the crabs that you catch? Is there a larger demand than the production of crabs?

4. What are the main features that distinguish one crab species from the other?

5. How much do you earn per day?

6. Do you use any chemicals to catch crabs? How does that affect the crab population?

7. What types of bait are used?

Budget

The budget introduces an estimate of how much your project or program idea is going to cost and is the financial plan you have estimated for the project.

The budget section refines your grant proposal with numbers. A well-crafted budget greatly adds to the reviewer's understanding of the project. The budget may be a simple one-page statement or may require a more complex presentation, such as a spreadsheet with projected support and revenue, notes explaining various items of expense or revenue, and detailed cost computations.

> ⚠ **Beware!**
> Make sure methods are compatible with the resources requested in the budget.

Usually, the greater the amount of money requested, the more detailed the budget. Typically the budget for private foundations is quite simple. Government-funding sources require considerable detail, and provide standard instructions and budget forms that must be used by all prospective applicants. Refer to the funder's guidelines for information on acceptable expenses and instructions on how to present the budget.

Keep in mind the funder's grant range as you develop your program and prepare the budget. To request an amount outside the range is an indication that you have not researched the funder thoroughly.

This section describes some of the typical elements of a budget. Note that not all proposals require all of these components and the level of detail varies from funder to funder and from project to project.

Check the Details

Although overhead expenses are often eligible for funding through government agencies, some set a maximum allowable percentage for indirect costs. After you have estimated your total direct expenses, you may be able to add a line item such as "Indirect costs at 15 percent of direct costs." In these cases, a budget detail usually is requested to indicate which items are included under indirect costs. For example, if you have included telephone charges as part of the agency's overall or indirect costs, you cannot also include telephone charges as a direct expense.

- *Project or program budget.* This refers to the income and expenses associated with the particular project for which you are seeking funding. Include income and expense projections.
- *Budget detail or justification.* This is also known as budget narrative. It includes details on certain income and expense items presented in the budget.
- *In-kind services.* These are also known as estimated donated goods. Sometimes not all costs have to be paid in cash. Donated goods and volunteer time are important to many nonprofit ventures. In-kind support refers to noncash, institutional assets that would have a cost attached to them if purchased outside the institution. If, for example, you receive a donated computer or have a volunteer receptionist, the costs of the program will be reduced.
- *Matching funds.* Some funding programs have a matching requirement, i.e., grantees must commit institutional resources as a condition of receiving a grant. The matching requirement can be found in the funder guidelines. A funder may require cash, in-kind support, or a combination of the two.
- *Fringe benefits.* These are benefits granted by an employer—such as a pension, a paid holiday, or health insurance— that have monetary value but do not affect basic wage rates. The fringe-benefit rates vary according to each organization. For example, at a university, the fringe-benefit rate is typically 28 percent during the academic year for full-time employees, and 8.0 percent for graduate students, part-time employees, and full-time employees during the summer.

> **Tip...**
>
> **Smart Tip**
> *Direct expenses* are non-personnel expenses that you would not incur if you did not do the project. They can be almost anything: travel; printing; space or equipment rental; supplies; insurance; or meeting expenses, such as food.

Project Expenses

Administrative or overhead expenses are nonpersonnel expenses you incur regardless of whether you do the project. For example, if you pay $500 a month for an office with space for four employees, you will continue to rent the office even if the project doesn't happen. But if the project does happen, one-quarter of the office space will be occupied by the project director. So you can apply for funding of one-quarter of your office rent, utilities, and administrative costs, such as phone, copying, postage, internet, and office supplies.

- *Direct costs*. These include personnel costs (i.e., salaries, benefits, and consultants fees) and materials needed to carry out the project (i.e., supplies, equipment, program-related travel, program-related rent, and printing costs).

- *Indirect costs or overhead costs*. These refer to expenses that are essential to all programs of the agency but are difficult to assign in specific amounts to any one program. They are costs that are shared

 Beware!
Many private funders do not allow indirect costs. So be sure to check the guidelines. If indirect costs are allowable, this portion of the grant generally goes to the institution to defray institutional overhead.

by the programs of an organization and can include auditing costs, the executive director's salary, general liability insurance, security, grounds, housekeeping, depreciation, and equipment leases.

Tips for Writing the Budget

- *Start early*. Get an early start in preparing your budget. Think about the day-in, day-out activities associated with your project. If there is an assessment at the end, leave sufficient time in your project timeline and financial resources for this phase.

- *Estimate the budget period*. Decide how much time the proposal covers, and develop a budget for that length of time. If your proposal is for a six-month project, the budget should demonstrate income and expenses for a six-month period; if your proposal is for a two-year project, the budget must show two years' worth of income and expenses.

- *Present a budget*. Generally, federal funders expect to see a budget—one in which income and expenses are equal or approximately equal. Most funders are

Balancing In-Kind

In-kind contributions are usually shown as income and expenses at the same levels. If, for example, you receive $3,000 worth of donated food from local merchants, you also "spend" or use $3,000 worth of donated food. If a volunteer teacher contributes $5,000 worth of her time, you also pay $5,000 in teaching expenses. Remember if you are showing in-kind contributions in your budget, they should be reflected as both revenue and expense.

reluctant to support programs that will end the funding period with either a large deficit or a major surplus of cash.

Sample of a Budget

Here is a sample of a basic budget submitted by an individual applicant to a private foundation. The grant request was to host a photographic exhibition.

Beware!
Balance your budget exactly. Don't pad the numbers or overestimate. If you put numbers in the budget in the same manner as throwing darts while blindfolded, it shows that you don't understand your project realistically.

Sample Budget

Estimated Budget

50 film rolls at $8 each	$400
Camera equipment	$3,000
Stationery expenses	$250
Postage costs	$250
Travel expenses to research site	$500
Total requested	**$4,400**

Here is an excerpt from a budget in a federal application:

	Cash Required	In-Kind Donations	Total
Expected Revenue			
Grants/foundations	$30,000		$30,000
Grants/government	$20,000		$20,000
Grants/corporations	$30,000		$30,000
Total revenue			**$80,000**

	Cash Required	In-Kind Donations	Total
Expected Expenses			
Salaries			
Program coordinator	$30,000		$30,000
Administrative assistant	$20,000		$20,000
Contract personnel	$10,000		$10,000
Program Services	$10,000	$5,000	$10,000
Total expenses	**$70,000**		**$65,000**

Evaluation and Dissemination

Evaluation and dissemination are the factors that give an indication whether or not the project has been successful. Although evaluation and dissemination are carried out at the end of the project, they need to be integrated into the project plan from the start.

Evaluation

Evaluation tells a funder whether you met your objectives, which in turn determines whether your program has been successful. Evaluations pinpoint what is really happening in your project so you can improve its efficiency, effectiveness, and equity.

From a funding agency's perspective, the evaluation determines whether its money was well-spent. From an applicant's perspective, an evaluation gives an indication as to whether the program is going well. With increasingly tight budgets, funders want to know that their dollars are not being wasted. This can be proven only when grant recipients are committed to evaluating their progress and outcomes. Most funders require award recipients to provide written reports on how the goals and objectives were met.

In order to conduct an evaluation, you need to gather information about whether your project reached its objectives. These measurement and evaluation tools are described in three ways:

1. *Data collection*. This section of the evaluation describes how and when you will collect information, what you want to find out, and where you will get the data you need.

Smart Tip

Tip...

The evaluation section is usually written after the need statement, goals, objectives, and methodology have been written, at the end of the program. However, they are integrated into the project plan from the start.

2. *Implementation.* This section describes what resources you need to ensure the project goals will be implemented and who is responsible for overseeing the evaluation.

3. *Use of evaluation results.* This section describes who will use the evaluation results as well as how and when the findings will be presented. You can also discuss what qualities your program had that contributed to its success (or failure).

Once you have the necessary data, there are different ways to conduct an evaluation, as explained below.

- *Internal evaluations.* An internal evaluation can be done by someone within your organization. This can be beneficial because an individual within your organization has great intuitive knowledge about your program and is less likely to be seen as an intruder. On the other hand, internal evaluations may be biased because of this close involvement with the program. Also, remember that there is a great deal of subjectivity involved in internal evaluations.

- *External evaluations.* External evaluations are conducted by people outside the organization, who often have a fresh perspective, can see the project differently, and bring considerable objectivity. On the other hand, external evaluations may be perceived as a threat by the staff and may require the evaluator to spend extra time understanding the program rationale.

- *Outcome evaluation or summative.* This examines the end result of a project. The goal here is to document the extent to which the project did what it was designed to do, and study the benefits, changes, or effects that occurred among

Proposal Outcome

The outcome evaluation occurs near or at the end of the project period. An outcome evaluation should produce an extensive narrative answering the following questions:

- ○ What did the project accomplish?
- ○ How many participants were impacted and in what way?
- ○ What overall difference did the project make?
- ○ Is the project worth funding again?
- ○ What methods did not go according to plan?

▲

the target population due to participation in the project. Outcomes are usually expressed in humanistic terms.

- *Process evaluation.* Conducted while the project is ongoing, a process evaluation generates information that will improve the project's effectiveness before it ends. Process evaluations systematically examine internal and external characteristics associated with the ongoing delivery and receipt of services.

- *Qualitative methods.* These are rooted in direct contact with the people involved in a project and involve three kinds of data collection: interviews, direct or field observation, and review of certain documents.

- *Impact evaluation.* These generate information to measure the overall worth and effect of the project beyond the grant period. An impact evaluation focuses on the project's larger value, such as the long-term fundamental change in participant's knowledge, attitudes, or behaviors. The project's effectiveness can be demonstrated among the target population, the community at large, and beyond.

- *Quantitative evaluation.* Quantitative methods translate experience into units that can be counted, compared, measured, and manipulated statistically. Quantitative methods are most appropriate when an evaluation aims to involve:
  - Understanding the quantities of particular aspects of a program;
  - Determining if a cause-and-effect relationship occurs;
  - Comparing two methods that are seeking the same outcomes; or
  - Completing any follow-ups at the post-project period.

Tips for Writing the Evaluation

Creating an evaluation is an important component of the program development process. It is neither a separate activity nor a function to be added after a program is complete. How a program will be evaluated must be determined before its implementation.

Here are some tips for writing evaluations:

- Describe why evaluation of the project is needed and what its purpose is. Project evaluations are conducted for various purposes. Here are some of the main reasons for evaluating:
  - To see if the program did what was expected
  - To see if the objectives and methods had an effec on the identified need
  - To maintain control over an ongoing project
  - To guide adjustments to an ongoing program to make it more effective
  - To obtain feedback from the target group

- Provide sufficient detail to demonstrate the technical soundness of all data collection instruments and procedures.

- Describe the information that is needed to complete the evaluation, the potential sources for this information, and the instruments that will be used for its collection.
- Identify and justify procedures for analysis, reporting, and utilization of the data.

Dissemination

Dissemination refers to the distribution of information. Evaluation is closely tied to dissemination. Funding sources frequently pay for disseminating the results of your grant project through one or more of the following mechanisms:

- A final report mailed to others in your field
- A quarterly journal
- A newsletter
- A seminar or conference on the topic
- Participation in national conferences
- A film, CD, or DVD presentation on the project

Dissemination helps to spread word of the project. It helps to increase public awareness of your program or project, pave the way for soliciting additional support, let others in your field know of your research findings (in the case of a research grant), and contribute to available information.

Tips for Writing the Dissemination

- *Include information why dissemination activities are important for your project.* For example, if you are conducting a research project on shark bites, producing a video about where they happen the most can serve as a warning for beach enthusiasts and provide information about what to avoid in the water.
- *Clearly identify the intended results of the dissemination effort.* The intended results of a project may include a journal publication, video documentary, or a web site among other sources. In some cases it is not possible to show specific results and final products. This is particularly true in the case of emergency grants, where it is not possible to show a final product as a result of medical bills being paid. In such grant applications there is no need to include a dissemination.
- *Specify precisely who will be responsible for dissemination and the person's qualifications.* For example, if a leading scholar in your university department is participating in the project, point to his post television appearances as examples of why he is qualified to promote the findings of the research project in the documentary series.
- *Discuss internal and external project dissemination.*

Sample Evaluation and Dissemination

Here is a sample evaluation and dissemination. Funds were requested to conduct a research project about Native American music and then publish a book.

Sample Evaluation and Dissemination

Evaluation and Dissemination

The project will be evaluated based on the number of people participating in the musical ensembles established at the healing center. Participants will be interviewed on a weekly basis. They will be asked questions about the musical events and what type of healing experiences they have had since the ensembles were established. Approximately 100 face-to-face interviews will be conducted with 30 participants.

The final products of the project will be a book, articles, and a web site. The research team has secured a publisher who has expressed an interest to sign a contract for the book titled *Healing through Native American Music.* Crown Publishers has agreed to publish it and market it at the national level. The book will also be made available in bookstores, libraries, universities, hospitals, and educational institutions throughout the United States. The research findings will also be submitted to magazines such as *Smithsonian , Journal of Ethnomusicology*, and *National Geographic*. The web site will make it possible for scholars throughout the world to gain access to the research findings. A project web site will be created titled "Native American Music and Healing."

Attachments

Funders may ask for a variety of attachments or supporting materials with the proposal. This section lists some of the items that are commonly used for attachments by nonprofit applicants. Having these items closely at hand saves time, energy, and resources for the grant writer and the nonprofit organization.

- A copy of the IRS letter that declares your organization tax exempt. If your group is not tax exempt, you may need to apply for grants through a fiscal agent or fiscal sponsor. In that case, send a copy of your fiscal agent's IRS letter.
- A list of the organization's board of directors and their qualifications, such as certified public accountant (CPA), marketing director, or bookkeeper.

- A financial statement from the organization's last complete fiscal year, including a statement of income and expenses as well as a balance sheet showing assets and liabilities at the end of the year. Some funders ask for an audited statement, which includes assets and liabilities.

- The organizational budget (not detailed program budgets) for the current fiscal year. If the application is submitted well into the fiscal year, also include a current financial statement showing actual year-to-date income and expenses next to budget projections.

- A budget for the next fiscal year if the application is submitted within three or four months of the new year.

- Any pertinent statistics about the organization (i.e., the number of people served, rankings, demographics). Include the most up-to-date.

- Newspaper articles. Funders generally like media attention and want to fund "winners." Newspaper articles describing your project or any awards or distinctions can add to your credibility.

- Letters of support to show that others value the project through an endorsement or as a formal partner.

- Financial data to demonstrate that the organization is financially stable and has good leadership.

- Any board minutes from meetings that are relevant to your project.

- The most recent form 990-PF (the tax return most nonprofits file with the IRS).

- The organization's bylaws, which serve as the internal "constitution," describing board powers and other basic legal matters.

- Three or four sentences of biographical information for key people, including the CEO, executive director, program director, and integral volunteers for the programs that are high priorities for grants.

- The organization's antidiscrimination policy for its workplace and services.

- The organization's mission statement.

- The organization's employer identification number (EIN)— the equivalent of an organization's Social Security number.

- The organization's DUNS (Data Universal Numbering System), which is required for all federal applications and increasingly requested by other government funders. You can apply for a DUNS number online at https://eupdate.dnb.com/requestoptions.html. Application takes about a month.

- An overall organization structure, with reporting arrangements.

- Job descriptions for all positions, including those in a new program.

- The number of the organization's full-time and part-time staff members, including volunteers when applicable.

Sample Organizational Resume

Hope International Mission Statement

A nonprofit organization dedicated to improving the economic, social, and cultural aspects of people living in developing countries.

Contacts

Board President: Jane Bren, 222 South Street, New Orleans, LA 00000

CEO: Sheila Kentsington, 335 North Avenue, New Orleans, LA 00000

History

The Eagle County Association selected Hope International to represent the county at The World Children's Day held in Geneva, Switzerland

Won a grant from the National Endowment for Humanities for helping children to read in developing countries

Eagle County Award for providing food for refugees in Somalia

Current Programs

A leading nonprofit in sending volunteers to Africa to feed the hungry

Working with women in India afflicted with AIDS

Resources

- Number of paid staff: 2
- Number of volunteers: 100
- Number of board members: 5
- Board meets: 7 times annually
- Total annual budget: $40,000

Where Our Funding Comes From

- 60% membership
- 10% corporate sponsorship
- 5% government grants
- 4% foundation grants

How We Use the Funding

- 10%: overhead costs
- 70%: humanitarian work in developing countries
- 10%: travel

- The organization's last annual report.
- A list of current, past, and potential sources of funding.
- An organizational resume, which acts as a marketing tool to highlight your organization's credentials and achievements. A sample organizational resume is on page 84.

> **Smart Tip**
> Check the funding agency's guidelines for any requested attachments before submitting your proposal. Note that some funders don't accept attachments.

Using Statistics to Support Your Project

Applicants are asked to use numbers and statistics to support the statement of need, goals, objectives, and methodology sections of a grant proposal. For social service, arts, and some environmental grants, the standard for statistical substantiation is not as rigorous as in academia or science. For most proposals of less than $100,000, two or three research sources are all you need to include.

> **Smart Tip**
> You don't need to spend months with your nose buried in books to find statistics to support your argument. The internet contains a wealth of information.

Before you start looking for research sources, consider exactly what kind of information you are seeking. Think about all the different kinds of numbers and statistics that might be useful to you. For example, if you are working for a children's literacy program, you might be able to use statistics about children, poverty, literacy, education, and volunteerism. If your program is statewide, you need population and school statistics for the state, as well as for the counties or towns where your program is expanding.

Questions to Consider When Finding Statistics for Your Project

To get started on your research, consider the following questions in relation to your program.

- What are some key words that describe the area of need or subject focus?
- What were the highlights of your conversation with your program director or the contact person? Did they give you any leads on statistics regarding the targeted community conditions?
- Has there been any recent media attention on the problem you project seeks to address?

- What is the geographic region—counties, states, etc.—you are covering?
- Do you have any reliable and up-to-date statistics already? Where did your existing material come from?
- Who at your organization might know where to get more?

Where to Find Statistics

Don't feel overwhelmed about finding statistics. If you know where to look, it is pretty easy to find surveys and statistical information. Here are some suggestions on where to start:

- *The internet.* The web makes it easy to do a broad survey of information about your field. Often you can download complete research papers or government reports that otherwise could take weeks to locate and order.

- *Newspapers.* Newspapers are a good place to start your search for community information. Some make their archives available online, but there can be a vast amount of published information that newspapers do not provide on their web sites and that you will need to find at the library.

   Larger regional and national papers often run stories with statistical tables or graphs alongside. For example, a newspaper might run a story about healing arts in the community that it serves. These kinds of news stories and sidebars can give you statistics as well as clue you in to what agencies and experts are working on the subject. Familiarize yourself with your regional newspaper's web site and how much information is available through online archives.

- *Government agencies.* There are dozens of federal and state agencies—from the *Department of Agriculture* to the *National Endowment for the Humanities*—that keep statistics on their subject areas and give the results out for free. Find an agency that is relevant for your field of interest, then call and ask general questions such as "I am studying the subject of music therapy among geriatric patients and wondered if anyone there keeps statistics about it."

- *Librarians.* Librarians can help you navigate the reams of information you may find on the internet, on library shelves, and in government reports. University librarians may specialize in specific topics.

Beware!

Be careful about the sourcing of statistics you find online. Remember that anyone can publish a web page and say anything they like. For your grant proposals, find the most credible information possible, for example, from government agencies, research institutes, and other reputable nonprofit organizations. Find one new and credible source of statistics on your subject area and bookmark it on your computer.

- *Scholars and other experts.* In all likelihood, someone in a university somewhere has spent most of his or her life researching exactly the kind of questions you are tackling. This person may have a great deal of information to share with you.

Submission Procedure

The method of submission varies with every funder. Some foundations specifically state that they accept applications only electronically, while others accept applications only through the mail. Hand-delivered applications are rare. Some foundations accept faxed applications. More and more federal funders are making courier delivery mandatory.

Applying for Grants Online

More and more funders are using the internet to post their guidelines and accept applications. Within the next ten years, the majority of funders are likely to make it mandatory to accept applications only online. Just as hand-written grant applications are now vintage, applications sent via regular mail in hard-copy format are likely to become obsolete.

Some funders post applications on their web sites. The format for online applications varies, but generally applicants have to register by creating a username and password. Typically, once

Smart Tip

Being internet-savvy gives you a distinct advantage when applying for grants. More and more funders are seeking "paperless" applications. This approach also reduces costs for the non-profit, which saves money on mailing out hard copies of applications.

The Faster the Better

Before September 11, 2001, the federal government discouraged overnight shipping of grant proposals by not providing all the information necessary for such shipping, such as a street address, phone number, etc. Since mail delivery, particularly in Washington, DC, has slowed for a new inspection process, the government now encourages overnight shipment and discourages the use of the U.S. Postal Service for time-sensitive materials. Courier delivery also is encouraged for security reasons.

▲

Shortcomings of Online Applications

There are some drawbacks in using online inquiries and applications:

○ There is no record of the submission being received, unless the funder acknowledges in writing that the application was received.

○ There may be unreliable connections to the server.

○ It may be harder for federal funders, particularly, who generally send applications for peer reviews.

○ Some funders have limits on the number of characters you can use in filling out an online form.

you have registered, you can start typing online and save the information as you go, meaning the next time you return to the application, your material is still there. You may also want to print what you have done, or copy and paste it into a word-processing document, so the work does not get lost.

E-Mail Etiquette

As mentioned earlier, electronic inquiries are becoming commonplace as people are becoming more accustomed to communicating via computer, cell phones, and YouTube. Although e-mails can be very informal, resist the temptation to be casual in your exchange. Maintain a professional approach and be concise. Write the e-mail as if you were writing a physical letter to the funder.

When sending e-mail submissions, confirm the address. If all you can find is a general e-mail, call the foundation and get the grant manager's direct address. Once you have one person's e-mail address at a funding source, you can generally use the same format to reach another person within the same organization. For example, both Dave Bret and Jane Dawson work at Charity Foundation. If Dave's e-mail is dave@charity foundation.net, it generally is safe to assume that Jane's e-mail is jane@charityfounda tion.net.

Subject lines can determine whether the reviewer actually reads your e-mail inquiry. Make sure the subject line relates to the content of the message. A "Hello" in the subject line is not likely to get a quick response, if any. A subject line such as "International grant request for AIDS awareness project" is more likely to get opened.

The content of your e-mail conveys information about your project as well as about you and your organization. The first thing a reader learns from your e-mail is your writing ability. If you misspell words or use incorrect phrases, the reader may assume you are uneducated or that you do not have the expertise to communicate effectively. Some funders may even feel insulted by such errors.

Within the body of the e-mail, describe your project. The challenge is to do so in a few paragraphs. Sometimes, instead of including the project information in the body of the e-mail, applicants are asked to attach a Microsoft Word document. No matter the format, be sure you include the following:

Formatting Tips for E-Mail Exchanges

Being aware of some basic formatting tips for e-mail exchanges can be useful. Some of them are:

- ○ Avoid being casual.
- ○ Write to a person, not to an office or department.
- ○ Address the person by name in the body of the e-mail. If you don't know the person, use Ms., Mr., or Dr.
- ○ Use a font that is easy to read.
- ○ Bold important headings for emphasis.
- ○ Don't use emoticons (smiley faces) or e-mail slang, such as LOL (laughed out loud).
- ○ Use proper grammar.
- ○ Run spellcheck.
- ○ Sign the e-mail with your full name and include your contact information. Many e-mail programs allow you to set up a default signature to be included at the end of every message. In your signature, be sure to include your:
  - – Full name and title
  - – The name of the applying organization
  - – Address
  - – Phone number
  - – Fax number
  - – Your e-mail address
  - – Your organization's web site address

- The need being addressed
- The clients served
- A project description
- The projected outcomes
- The program duration

> **Smart Tip** Tip...
>
> Read your e-mail a few times before you send it. Save copies of all e-mail exchanges in a folder with the funder's name.

The most important statements should appear early in the e-mail. Details can follow in subsequent paragraphs. Remember to include the organization's web address. This will be helpful if the funder needs additional background on your agency. Use attachments if you need to send supporting information. In general, an attachment that is larger than 50KB may be hard to download. How to send attachments varies with each funder. Some may want them broken to smaller files, while others will want everything in one single e-mail.

Applying for Grants through the Mail

If you are sending a grant application via regular mail, and your application is more than three pages long, use 8.5-by-11-inch envelopes. Have a stack of large-size envelopes handy so you don't have to rush to the office supply store every time you mail out an application. Sometimes you may need bubble mailers, too.

A clean looking, neatly packaged application gives the impression of a well-organized, successful organization, whereas an envelope full of pieces of paper without any order gives the opposite impression. While neatness is important to foundations, a showy, expensive-looking look does not help your proposal. Avoid three-ring binders, spiral binders, colored charts and graphs, and embossed folders.

> **! Beware!**
>
> Pay attention to the postmark date. Some funders indicate that they will accept a postmark date for the deadline. Be sure to read a funder's guidelines carefully and note whether they state "must arrive by" the date or "must be postmarked by" the date. If the project must be postmarked by a predetermined date, you must mail your application via the U.S. Postal Service. Marks made by other delivery providers will not fulfill this requirement.

Schedule Your Submissions

Many foundations fund grants only at certain times of the calendar or fiscal year. Become familiar with the funding schedules for the foundations in which you are interested and coordinate your submissions with their timetables. Make sure you complete your application in time to meet the funder's deadlines. Nothing is worse than preparing a submission and missing the deadline by a week.

Don't Become a Gadfly

After submitting your application, avoid contacting the foundation to inquire about your application status. Most foundations are understaffed and constantly bothering the funder can actually work against your application. Once an application is mailed, let it go and move on to the next application. Detachment is far healthier than attachment.

Because some funders may take up to a year from the deadline date to make the award decisions, be patient. During the review period, little if any contact is made with the applicants. Hurrying the grant process is like waiting to reap summer tomatoes the minute the seeds have been planted. You don't have to be an experienced gardener to know that seeds take time and specific weather conditions to grow and bear fruit. Visiting the garden every morning does not necessarily speed the growth of seeds. Imagine the grant application as the seed. Once it has been planted at the funder's site, it has to undergo several processes in the growth stage. Several reviewers look at your application and finally decide whether it should be funded.

Proposal List for Nonprofits

Here are some sample requirements for a grant application submitted by a nonprofit. The points below need to be incorporated into the elements of a grant proposal.

Section I: Your agency's background, including:

- The mission
- The founding date
- The major programs
- The number and capacity of staff
- Any links with similar organizations

Section II: The project you propose, including:

- The specific community need you will address
- Your project goals and objectives
- The ways you propose to tackle the problem
- Expected immediate and long-term results
- How many people, and who, will be served
- The contribution your project will make to the community
- Why your organization wants to pursue this particular project
- A list of other organizations that provide a similar service
- The expected contribution to knowledge and experience in the field

- The relationship to your agency's overall program
- Any available professional support

Section III: Your project implementation plan, including:
- Your timeline: steps to be taken, by whom and when
- Names of cooperating organizations
- A list of the project staff, consultants, volunteers
- Any participating advisory groups

Section IV: Project continuation, including:
- Any plans to continue work as an ongoing project after the funding period
- Any future funding sources
- Other current funding sources

Section V: Project evaluation, including:
- Your criteria for effectiveness
- What type of evaluation method will be used
- Your methods and schedule for measuring short- and long-term results
- Who will assess the results

Section VI: Financial information, including:
- A line-item income and expense budget for the project
- Budget narrative
- The amount your organization will contribute to the project
- A list of other foundations to which you have submitted this proposal
- An indication of whether funds have been committed, declined, or are pending
- Your organization's current annual operating budget

Here is an example of the grant guidelines provided by a nonprofit:

The Dorothy Madden Arts Grants Program

Who can apply: Nonprofit organizations with a focus on the arts are eligible to apply. Qualifying fields are music, sculpture, writing, painting, puppetry, and dance. Photographers are not qualified for this grant program.

The proposal narrative should be ten pages in length, describing the type of artists served by your nonprofit, exhibitions held, budget, recent awards, and board members.

In a separate page include the budget for the requested grant funds. Include complete computations of salary payments for participating staff members.

The methodology section should include details about how the art project will be carried out, timeline, and participants.

Supporting materials should include your most recent audited financial statements, any awards, media publicity pertaining to your nonprofit, list of board members with their contact information and qualifications, IRS determination letter, and other pertinent information.

Proposal List for Individuals

Before submitting your individual proposal, check this list to be sure you've covered all your points. Note that this is an application checklist required by a federal funder. Include the original (unbound, one sided) 40-page narrative and 12 collated copies in this order:

- Signed application cover sheet
- Statement of significance and impact
- Table of contents
- List of project participants
- Narrative
- Budget forms
- Appendices
- History of grants
- List of evaluators

Plus

- Two copies of the suggested list of evaluators
- Resumes of principal project personnel
- Videos demonstrating the existing research
- One extra copy of the list of project participants
- SASE (self-addressed stamped envelope) to confirm receipt of application
- SASE for any materials that you want returned to you
- Label each accompanying document with the applicant's name, address, and e-mail address. On the narrative, leave a one-inch margin from the top and bottom. Use double spacing, Times New Roman font style, no smaller than 11 points.

There are a few different details regarding emergency grants. They usually don't require an evaluation section in the narrative, as it is the immediate need of a person that is being addressed. Most emergency funders require a one page description of the need at hand and why funds are being requested. Supporting documents proving the need are a must. For example, if funds are being requested to pay medical bills, then copies of doctor visits, hospitalization bills, and pharmaceutical products are required as proof.

7

Alternative
Forms of
Approach

Some funders ask for a letter of inquiry (LOI), or a concept paper, instead of a traditional long proposal. The elements to include in a LOI or concept paper are similar to the long proposal, although some variations may apply.

Letter of Inquiry (LOI)

The LOI is the most common first approach in grant writing. In fact, many funding sources require applicants to submit a letter of inquiry before they discuss the project further. Through a LOI, you are asking whether the funder has an interest in your project and sufficient interest to invite a full proposal. Typically, a LOI should be between one and two pages.

Even though an LOI is not considered a full proposal, it contains much of the same information. An LOI clearly and concisely describes the project, its aims, its significance, its duration, and the amount of money requested. An LOI should be a succinct and compelling summary of the program plans.

An LOI is good for the funder as it gives the opportunity to quickly review a project idea at a glance. This can save potentially hundreds of hours of reviewing in the case of projects that fail to meet the funder guidelines. If the letter of inquiry appears to interest the funder, a more detailed proposal can be requested. For the nonprofit, the development of a good LOI generates confidence and enthusiasm. The requirements of an LOI force the grant writer and the organization to think ahead and realistically assess the organization's capabilities and plans. The letter also forces you to link the funder's interests with the applicants.

LOIs can often take as much time to write as a long proposal does. Even though an LOI is short, it must undergo extensive preparation and revision. Don't assume that you can write an LOI in ten minutes because of its brevity. It requires intensive editing, just like your proposal does.

The Elements of a Letter of Inquiry

In a LOI the following should be addressed, although the requirements may vary with each funder:

- What problem does your project address? Why is this issue significant?
- What strengths and skills do you/your organization have to bring to this project? What makes you the right person to conduct it?
- What are the key personnel, and briefly, what are their qualifications?
- What results do you expect, both immediate and long term?
- What plans do you have to disseminate information about your project?
- How much money are you requesting?
- What is the timeline for the project?
- What is your method of evaluation?

- Who will lead the project?

You should always review a funder's guidelines when writing a LOI. However, the most common elements of a letter of inquiry are described in this section. (For more detailed information, see "The Elements of a Grant Proposal" in Chapter 6.)

- *Opening paragraph.* The letter's opening paragraph summarizes the document and addresses your request. The introduction should describe what you are proposing to do, how much money you are requesting, and the duration of the project.

- *Statement of need.* An LOI's statement of need must address the following points as briefly as possible:
  - Who is affected by the problem and why it is important
  - What your organization and other agencies are doing currently to address the problem and what remains to be done
  - What factors contribute to the existence of the problem
  - What consequences the target population will face if the need is not met
  - What outcomes you hope to achieve
  - Any pertinent statistics or research

- *Organizational description.* In this paragraph, include a short history of the organization, its mission, and its qualifications. Funders want to know that they are dealing with a stable and well-regarded organization that manages money wisely. Mention prior successes with projects similar to the one you are proposing. If you have room, you may also want to include a brief statement about the organization's clientele; staff; ability to see the project through; and major, recent accomplishments and goals. Make sure the length of your organizational description is proportional to the rest of your LOI.

- *Description of the project.* While this should not be a detailed description, use your space wisely to give the reader a clear sense of the scope of the project. Include information about the population you are targeting, how many participants are involved, the goals and objectives; the main methods, the length of the project, and anticipated starting and ending dates.

- *Budget request and information.* It is not necessary to include detailed financial information in a letter of inquiry. Simply estimate the project's total cost during a certain time period and indicate how much of that you will be requesting.

- *Closing statement.* End the LOI by reiterating the project's purpose, potential impact, and alignment with the funder's interest. Suggest an appropriate follow-up method within a certain period of time. Close the letter by thanking the funder for her attention.

- *Attachments.* Foundations may request an annual financial report and proof of the organization's 501(c)(3) or nonprofit status to ensure grant eligibility. (For more information, see the section "Attachments" in Chapter 6.)

▲

- *Signature.* Get the highest ranking member of the organization to sign the letter.

Sample Letter of Inquiry

The contents, format, and length of a LOI vary with every application. The sample LOI below was a project proposal submitted by The Children's Health Project to the Conservation Food and Health Foundation in Massachusetts. The address in Dorchester is not correct. The project has now ended.

Sample Letter of Inquiry

Mary Beth Birnbaum, Director
The Food for Children Foundation
Dorchester, MA 00000

Mr. Charles Seaborn, Grants Manager
Conservation, Food and Health Foundation
Goodwish Avenue
Millneck, NY 00000

Dear Sir/Madam:

Green Living: Introducing Healthy Foods to School Cafeteria Plans

Introduction: The focus on healthy living and "going green" has never been greater. People are regaining an appreciation for the age-old belief that what we eat is directly related to how we feel, look, and age. The emphasis on healthy cuisine is penetrating into schools as well. The Children's Health Project proposes to start a workshop series that transports healthy foods to children in South Dakota. It plans to conduct fifty workshops and requests $25,000 to carry them out. The project will take place from May 2008–April 2009.

The Need: The problem that the Children's Health Project seeks to address is the growing habit of introducing trans fat foods to school cafeteria plans, thereby making obesity a major health concern in American schools. Those mostly affected by this problem are school children K–12. Factors contributing to the existence of this problem include the lack of awareness about healthy foods, cheap pricing of trans fat foods that are promoted in schools, and self interests of food companies that promote their products that may not necessarily be in the best interests of school children.

The Children's Health Project currently visits schools and meets with administrators to introduce new food menus, conduct surveys about weight issues affecting children, and introduces healthy diets into the school curriculum.

By conducting fifty workshops, we hope to make adjustments in menu plans to contribute towards a more wholesome diet throughout schools in Dorchester, Massachusetts. Green salads, herbs, vegetable soups, and fruits will be the focus of these workshops. The overall expected outcome is to expose school children to healthy foods.

Organizational Description: The Children's Health Project was established in 2001 under the umbrella organization of the Children's Health Foundation. It addresses health and nutrition concerns of children in K-12 in schools throughout Dorchester, Massachusetts.

Attachments: included are our annual financial report and board member affiliations. Press releases and media publicity about the Children's Health Project have also been included.

Concluding Remarks: I would like to emphasize that currently our organization is one of the few that works directly with the foods reaching school children. Introducing healthy foods to school cafeteria plans can lead to a healthier generation of youth and adults in the years to come.

Thank you.

Sincerely yours,

Mary Beth Birnbaum

Mary Beth Birnbaum, Director

Concept Paper

A concept paper is a short grant proposal and is typically between two and five pages. Concept papers provide a way to obtain informal feedback on your idea before you spend the time and energy required to create a full proposal for formal submission.

Concept papers are ideal for projects that are fairly well developed yet still able to be shaped based on the funder's feeback. Serving as a starting point for a discussion, concept papers can be used to draw in the funder; solicit their feedback and advice; and create investment in an idea.

> ## Smart Tip
>
> One of the biggest advantages of using a concept paper as a first approach is that it can be sent to a number of potential funding sources accompanied by a customized letter. The disadvantage of a concept paper is that it may not include enough detail to make a strong case to the funder.

The Elements of a Concept Paper

Although concept papers vary in content, length, and components, the following information is generally included:

- *Title*. The title should be easy to understand and accurately reflect the goals of your project. When writing a title, choose one that is easy to digest. Avoid trendy or ostentatious words, and check to make sure you are not choosing a title already being used by others.

- *Introduction*. The introduction provides an overview of the idea, gives shape to the rest of the document, and summarizes the key points. Include a sentence stating what you are seeking and why; discuss the purpose of the project. These first few sentences should be compelling so the reader wants to continue.

- *Statement of need*. Briefly describe the problem you seek to address, the population you hope to serve, and the importance of the issue. Do not assume the reader understands the situation. Provide enough detail to substantiate your claims. Talk about other efforts to solve the problem and how your project fills a gap in services or knowledge.

- *Budget*. Outline the amount of money you are seeking and for what time period. Indicate if the money is directly related to the project, overhead staff and salary, travel, or any other categorized expense.

- *Organizational description*. Acknowledge your organization's capabilities and its capacity to achieve the stated goals. Mention awards, honors, and merits your organization has achieved in the past five years.

- *Project description*. Briefly describe what you propose to do and highlight the innovation in your approach. Give time frames for implementation of the project. Describe any agencies that will be partners for the project.
- *Summary*. The closing summary reiterates the importance and purpose of the project as well as the impact it will have.

Sample Concept Paper

Take a look at the sample concept paper below created by an international foundation, seeking assistance from a U.S. foundation.

Sample Concept Paper

Rain Water Harvest Tanks in Sri Lanka

Introduction: The Women's Foundation is seeking funds to build rain water harvest tanks in the town of Anuradhapura, Sri Lanka. Anuradhapura experiences one of the worst droughts in the country every year. The shortage of water disrupts the day-to-day lifestyle of the local people.

Statement of Need: According to the Ministry of Health, only 27% of the people of Sri Lanka have a pipe borne water supply. The drought in Anuradhapura devastates people, animals, trees, and irrigation systems. Diseases are rampant as clean water is scarce. Women are often seen carrying gallons of water for miles in the scorching heat.

During the drought months, the local government supplies clean water to public places twice a week. Each family is given three barrels of water for free. They have to conserve this quota for cooking, washing, and other purposes.

During the drought, lucrative private companies make handsome sums of money by selling water at exorbitant prices. Affluent villagers purchase additional water. Poverty-stricken families, on the other hand, pawn their jewelry and other valuables to buy additional water.

Efforts to address the issue of water scarcity include education workshops on preserving water at home, recycling water, and introducing faucets that help to preserve water. By building twenty rain water harvest tanks in Anuradhapura, The Women's Foundation seeks to provide clean water to approximately 100,000 people in Anuradhapura and surrounding areas. The idea of building rain water harvest tanks is different from existing programs as it addresses the problem at the root level and offers a practical solution. Building rain water harvest tanks is a simple strategy that will benefit thousands of people simultaneously.

Project Description: The Women's Foundation wants to preserve freely available rain water so that villagers can use it during the drought. A rain water harvest tank is an oval-shaped well, built above the ground. According to this simple water storing technique, rain water during the monsoon is funneled through pipes directly into tanks. One rain water harvest tank is able to sustain the daily needs of one hundred people for several days. A rain water harvest tank is a permanent structure that stores water during the rainy season and distributes when necessary.

The Women's Foundation proposes the construction of 20 rain water harvest tanks. They will be close to strategic public places like hospitals, libraries, bus stops, and schools.

Each rain water harvest tank costs $400 to build. The total requested is $8,000. The funding will be used between January 2008 and December 2008.

Organizational Description: The Women's Foundation was founded in 1985 as a response to the needs of women in Sri Lanka. The Women's Foundation is dedicated to improving the economic, social, and educational lives of the local people. Our staff consists of four full time individuals and three hundred volunteers. In 2005 The Women's Foundation was voted the most influential nonprofit in our area and won a medal of honor for its services. Past accomplishments include a fruit jam project, counseling center for pregnant teenagers, environmental clean-up projects, and teaching English as a second language.

Conclusion: Rain water harvest tanks will be an invaluable resource to the people of Anuradhapura. Lifting the scarcity of water will improve the economic, social, and educational aspects of the people. The Women's Foundation would like you to consider investing in this eco-friendly project.

Thank you.

Wendy Matthew, Executive Director
The Women's Foundation

Effective
Grant-Writing
Techniques

Learning to write a cohesive and persuasive grant proposal is crucial. Writing is the medium through which you communicate with your funder, and your work can determine whether your grant request gets funded. Here are some tips to improve your writing skills.

Avoid Jargon

Avoid unnecessary words and redundancy. They waste your space, waste the reviewer's precious time, and may confuse the reader. Never send your reader to the dictionary by using uncommon and unfamiliar vocabulary. Whatever you plan to write, say it once and say it right.

Using language that is used by a particular group, profession, or culture—especially when the words and phrases are highly technical—can be a disadvantage. Jargon also can convey a sense of pretentiousness and meaninglessness. If you must use a technical term, define it when you first use it.

Here is an example of a sentence that uses jargon:

The Fresnel lens that was invented in 1822 revolutionized the study of pharalogy.

If the reviewer does not know what a Fresnel lens is or what pharology means, your point and its significance is lost. You are making the reviewer's job more difficult by using jargon.

Instead of being too specific about the Fresnel lens, which is a type of illumination introduced to lighthouses by France in the 18th century, and using the word "pharalogy" which is a reference to people who study lighthouses (the word comes from the first recorded lighthouse in history, the Pharos Lighthouse of Alexandria around 290 B.C.), this sentence can be re-structured so as to avoid jargon:

The invention of the Fresnel lens, which was a type of illumination used in lighthouses in the 18th century, revolutionized the study of lighthouses.

Explain Acronyms

You cannot assume that readers know the same acronyms or buzzwords that are common to your organization or field of interest. While readers may understand that "HUD" refers to the U.S. Department of Housing and Urban Development, a self-coined acronym such as "CARA"—an abbreviation for the Connecticut Arts Response Action—can confuse the reader. Make yourself clear. Give readers the full name or title on first reference, followed by the acronym in parentheses.

Write Short Sentences

A sentence provides clarity when it is brief. When sentences get too long, wordiness creeps in, making it easy for readers to get lost in the phrases and lose their train of thought. By the end of the sentence, the reader may have forgotten what was written at the beginning. Eliminate wordiness, as it is likely to lead to grammatical errors. Take a look at the following sentence:

"Give Peace a Chance," which will take place in fall 2008, will be a photographic exhibition depicting images of conflict from around the world, and the images will be displayed in bus stations, libraries, and coffee shops, where the predicted audience will be the general public involved in their day-to-day activities.

Here is how you can express the thoughts more clearly:

"Give Peace a Chance" will be a photographic exhibition on world peace and harmony. The images will be displayed in bus stations, libraries, and coffee shops. The predicted audience will be the general public pursuing their day-to-day activities. The project will take place in fall 2008.

Write Cohesively

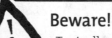

Beware!
Typically a sentence in a grant proposal needs to be fewer than 20 words. If a sentence has 50 words, it most likely needs revision.

Organize your thoughts clearly. Cohesion is key. Arrange the elements of your thoughts in a way that creates structure within the proposal. This forces you to eliminate unnecessary details that that can lead to a disconnected proposal.

Make your sentences short and powerful. Repeating the same points may lead the funder to believe that your project lacks substance, just as your writing does.

The following is an example where the thoughts are disjointed. The request is being made by an individual for funding for a photographic project:

I will be visiting Varanasi, India, to conduct a photographic documentary on Varanasi, India. I want to show how old ideas exist with modern trends. It is one of the oldest living cities in the world. It captures the essence of India.

Here is how you can organize your thoughts better:

Varanasi, India, is one of the oldest living cities in the world. In many ways, Varanasi captures the essence of India—filled with contrasts between the old order and the new; ancient civilizations and contemporary globalization; and the sacred and the secular. My goal is to conduct a photojournalism project titled "Tradition vs Modernism in Varanasi, India." The theme of the photo project will be to study how traditional rituals are being assailed and benefited by modernism and globalization.

Avoid Expressions of Uncertainty

The language in a grant proposal needs to be authoritative. Words and sentences such as "may," "basically," "it appears to me," and "I might be able to," show uncertainty on the part of the applicant. Such phrases leave the reader to wonder whether the applicant has the capacity to carry out the project successfully. The following is an example of a sentence expressing uncertainty:

It appears to me that there is a shortage of juried exhibitions presenting shows on war veterans, I think.

You can revise this sentence to be more authoritative, as follows:

Fewer than 30 percent of juried photographic exhibitions have themes on war veterans.

Avoid Using "the Former" and "the Latter"

Using the words "former" and "latter" slows down the reader. Some reviewers may have to re-read the previous text to determine what was "former" and what was "latter." Here is an example:

Trans-fat foods in public schools have led to unhealthy eating while green salads, although less popular, add nutritional value to meals. There is a national effort to eliminate the former and increase the latter food type.

The following sentences more clearly convey the message:

Although many schools around the country continue to use trans fats, there is a push to replace them with green salads. Salads are considered healthier and add more nutritional value to meals.

Get Rid of Emotional Language

A little amount of emotion may be helpful in grant proposals but too much is likely to ruin your chances of winning a grant. Funders are generally convinced by facts, not emotional statements. Although most people are sensitive and can be swayed by emotions, too much emotional writing can be a disqualification.

Emotional sentences are referred to as "puny." They communicate your project through feelings, not through facts. Lamenting about your mortgage, unpaid utilities, and ill health generally is not be the best strategy to crafting a proposal.

The following is an example of puny language:

Our board feels that the establishment of gallery space is a wonderful idea. It will give local people the opportunity to display their fascinating works of art. Unfortunately, though, the recent loss of our executive director who died of a terminal illness, the fire that destroyed our office space, and an increase in rent have crushed our organization financially. We are trapped in a sad situation and truly need your help.

This can be more appropriately worded as follows:

The establishment of a gallery space will enable local artists to display their work free of charge. It will also bring our arts council a monthly income through juried art shows, entry fees, and the sale of art work, thereby enabling our organization to advance financially.

Avoid Claims of Being the "Best"

Avoid superlatives in your grant proposal. You are less likely to be challenged if you write "Method X is a good way to reduce teen pregnancies," than if you write "Method X is the best way to reduce teen pregnancies."

Avoid Tag Questions

A "tag" is a short question that is added to the end of a sentence or command. We are used to adding tags in conversations, such as "You mailed the greeting cards to the client, right?"

However, when it comes to grant proposals, there is only one thing to do with tag questions: delete them. Here is an example of a tag question:

Public art is one of the most ubiquitous forms of art, don't you agree?

In agrant proposal, the above sentence needs to be rephrased, as follows:

Public art is one of the most ubiquitous forms of art.

Spell, Style, and Grammar Checkers

Checkers can be a useful tool for grant writers, but they should be used with discretion. Spell, style, and grammar checkers generally are integrated into word-processing programs. Some of these programs automatically alert you to a misspelled word or grammatically incorrect phrase as you type. Word-processing programs can generally check for the following types of incorrect or poor usage:

- Sentences that are too long
- Paragraphs that are too long
- Passive versus active verb constructions
- Adjacent duplicate words
- Vague phrases
- Incorrect punctuation
- Missing spaces
- Too many spaces between words/sentences
- Overused words

Don't Disappoint the Reader

Be aware that a heading, subheading, or topic sentence is essentially a promise to the reader about what is in the text that follows. Remember to address these points—to keep your promise. For example, if you say "The chart below gives an indication of how many elderly residents in nursing homes have experienced injuries from falls at Sunny Hill Nursing Home in 2007," but there isn't a chart, you are betraying the reader.

Don't Blow Your Own Horn

Avoid an undue amount of self-praise. Let your data speak for you. Avoid statements such as: "Our outstanding and exceptional method" or "Our organization is the best."

Smart Tip

Tip...

Remember the adage, "'Tis the empty can that makes more noise." Similarly, don't brag about your project as being the best. This approach might work against you. Show substance in your achievements and allow them to speak for you.

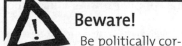

Be Politically Correct

Be politically correct, particularly when you are discussing individuals. Say "people with disabilities," not "disabled people." Use "minority individuals," or terms such as African American or Native American when you have to be specific about ethnicity. Use inclusive, nonsexist language by substituting she/he and his/her.

> **⚠ Beware!**
> Be politically correct when crafting grant proposals. Terms such as "people of color" or "minority individuals" are safer than "colored people"; "developing countries" sounds better than "third world."

Avoid Using Modifiers

Examples of modifiers include "very," "really," and "certainly." Use these sparingly in your proposal. Using them frequently is an indication that you have a limited vocabulary. Using excessive modifiers also indicates your insecurity in relying on simplicity.

The following is an example using a modifier:

The Center for Organic Foods, which is an extremely credible organization in the industry promotes a very important message about eating very healthy foods.

A more effective way of writing it is as follows:

The Center for Organic Foods plays a strategic role in raising awareness about eating healthy foods.

Using Metaphors to Strengthen Your Argument

A metaphor is a figure of speech that enhances the meaning of a sentence with colorful imagery. In grant writing the use of metaphors can enhance the meaning of a sentence with colorful imagery and create a written painting with words. Notice how the plainness of writing in the sentence below is adorned by the addition of a metaphor:

Despite the ongoing peace treaty, several signs have indicated that the country is moving into unsteady territory. War can erupt at any moment.

▲

An example of using a metaphor is:

The peace treaty is hanging by a thread.

Create a Visual Painting with Your Words

When your paragraphs create images appealing to the visual, aural, and gustatory senses, the reviewer is enticed to read your proposal further. The longer a funder lingers on your proposal, the more, likely your project is to be funded. Adopt an arresting writing style that grabs readers attention and makes them want to keep reading.

The first writing style is plain, boring, and lacks personality:

"Aroma" derives from the Greek word for spice. "Aromatherapy" means 'treatment using scents.' It refers to the use of essential oils in holistic healing to improve one's health and emotional well-being and to restore balance in the body. Fragrant essential oils can enrich one's life, whether they are used therapeutically, in beauty treatments, to perfume a spa, or for sheer pleasure.

The Lotus Spa wants to use aromatherapy treatments to improve the well-being of people.

The following is an example of writing that makes the reader want to visit a spa:

Aromatherapy massage is as relaxing to give as it is to receive. The ancient Egyptians and Greeks greatly appreciated fragrance. Cleopatra is said to have indulged in herbal essences as part of her beauty regimen and healthy lifestyle.

The goal of my project is to promote aromatherapy massage as a healer. Lotus Spa will produce herbal essences that are healthy for the skin. Concentrated essences extracted from plants have been valued throughout history for their therapeutic properties.

Lotus Spa will incorporate a wide variety of essential oils into massage treatments. Basic massage strokes such as fan stroking, kneading, and circular pressures work effectively in aromatherapy massage. Massage with aromatic oils softens the skin and aids healing. Some of the herbs used to create essential oils are juniper, lavender, geranium, marjoram, and rosemary. Lotus Spa will offer clients an array of choices on aromatherapy massage, fragrance products, and healing methods.

Stick to One Tense

Avoid changing tenses within the proposal. Using present tense in one section and the past tense in another can confuse the reader. Here is an example:

A CD recording of the music helped to increase awareness of the different types of singing found on Native American reservations. The CD was released in record stores last week. The recording is helpful to schoolchildren. It was also helpful to musicians, healers, and scholars. School children are listening to the CD in the classrooms.

Notice how much easier this is to understand when just one tense is used.

A CD recording of the music helped to increase awareness of the different types of singing on Native American reservations. The CD has been widely received by schoolchildren, musicians, healers, and scholars.

Say What You Mean, Get What You Want

Be direct in your proposal. Don't beat around the bush and write vague ideas. Tell the funder directly what you are looking for. Clearly identify your objectives and state your specific needs. Describe how the grant maker might help you solve your problems. Be direct and succinct, but remain persuasive.

The first example doesn't make its point to the reader:

There are very few outlets available for treating the disease of alcoholism in Sri Lanka. This is a taboo topic where very few are informed about the disease concept of alcoholism. Having a recovery center and support groups can be of great benefit for creating sober living groups.

Here is an example of writing directly to the funder instead of being vague about the project:

The current outlets available for alcoholics and their families in Sri Lanka are virtually nonexistent. Alcoholism is seen as a moral weakness, a lack of willpower, and an obsession of the devil. My goal is to start an alcohol treatment center that educates people about the disease concept of alcoholism and offers treatment programs for those seeking recovery.

My mission is to start an alcohol treatment facility named Sober Living. It will organize daily Alcoholic Anonymous (AA) meetings; present symposia for medical practitioners and mental health professionals about understanding alcoholism as a treatable disease; offer independent outpatient programs for alcoholics and their families interested in recovery; and provide recovery programs for families crippled by alcoholic members.

Document Your Case

When discussing the problem you intend to solve, go beyond merely describing its existence. Prove that it exists through statistics, case studies, testimony, and other measurable data. Numbers are better than vague opinions; use sound judgment about the information you present. Give the reader hope, so your proposal does not sound like a lost cause. Replace opinion modifiers with quantitative modifiers. For example, replace "most" or "many" with "between 50 and 60 percent."

Give Your Grant Proposal the Human Touch

Don't be too technical and dense in your proposal writing style. This can be a turn-off to the reviewer. It is up to the grant writer to reach human feelings through writing: use anecdotes; provide real-life examples; supply quotes from those who have benefited or will benefit from your services; include photos; emphasize the needs of those you serve, not your own; and describe the situation in terms that are factual and carry human interest.

Read the paragraphs below and in contrast, see how the human connection has been better established in the ensuing example.

The tsunami claimed over 350,000 lives on December 26th, 2004. Sri Lanka was one of the worst affected countries. After visiting with thousands of tsunami victims and listening to their needs, our organization realized the importance of archiving these tsunami stories.

Here is an excerpt from a proposal submitted by an aid organization to documenting stories of tsunami survivors in Sri Lanka:

Three years have passed since the tsunami claimed more than 350,000 lives in 11 countries across Asia and Africa. Sri Lanka was one of the worst affected, with more than 60,000 recorded deaths and thousands more missing. Our organization was one of the first to arrive at the disaster scene. Stories of sadness and woe filled our ears:

It was December 26, 2004. In the distance, I heard a child screaming, "The sea is coming! The sea is coming! Run!" I turned around and became numb at what I saw. Blinking twice to make sure it was not double vision, I ran for dear life. I had never seen anything like it. The water was pitch black, boiling hot, and it slammed at me like an ugly monster. The wave was 30-feet tall, and claimed everything and everyone around its path. It made a thundering roar and drowned every other noise around me. I knew I could not save both my children. I held on to my five-year-old daughter and placed my two-month-old baby in a styrofoam box that I use to store fish. Because the box is light, it floats. Three days later, a villager found the box on a tree with my baby safe and alive.

Everyone has a desire to be heard. Our organization listens to the economic, social, and educational needs of the Sri Lankan people. Our present focus is to record, document, and archive the real-life stories of tsunami survivors in Sri Lanka.

Tsunami Stories: An Ethnography *will be a series of documented stories of 500 tsunami survivors in Sri Lanka."*

Sample Project Description Using Effective Grant-Writing Techniques

Here is a project description that was funded by a private foundation. Some of the writing techniques discussed in this chapter can be found in this description:

Living in a Box

Did you know that there are approximately 32 million people in the United States awaiting death row? That is right. 32 million alcoholics await execution through the lethal drug. Alcohol claims one out of 10 people in the United States and is the number-one drug killer.

During the last thirty years there has been a general understanding in the United States that alcoholism is a progressive, family disease, and that it is treatable. This medical advancement has transformed lives of alcoholics and their families to step outside of their self-inflicted cells and to enjoy things in life besides alcohol. Unfortunately, the majority of alcoholics and their families live in denial and transmit dysfunctional elements caused by the disease to the next generation.

What's more, families living with alcoholics unconsciously become enablers, who assist their loved ones to continue drinking. Their codependencies have subconsciously shaped them to enable the drinking patterns and to cover up for the after effects of such behavior.

Living in a box will be a public art project that will be carried out at Madison Public Park next summer. It will give visual representation to the insanity caused

▲

by alcoholism and how the disease of alcoholism shrinks the world of alcoholics into cells over a period of time. The goal of the public art project is to inspire alcoholics and their families to take the first step towards recovery, and that is to stop living in denial about the disease.

Congratulations!
You've Been Awarded a Grant

It is exciting to receive the long-awaited letter saying you have won a grant. After all the hard work, resources, and enthusiasm that were invested into the preparation of the application, your reward has come.

Here is a sample acceptance letter:

Sample Acceptance Letter

Dear Angelina Lambert,

Congratulations! We are pleased to announce that you have been selected as a grant recipient for our 2008 grant cycle. We have enclosed a check for the sum of $35,000 toward the research project to be conducted in Greece. By cashing this check, you agree to use the funds for the charitable purposes outlined in your proposal.

Please contact us if you have any questions or if we can assist you further. We wish you the very best success in your artistic work.

Sincerely,

World Heritage and Archive Foundation

It is important to remember that getting the award check is not the end of the journey. Rather, receiving the check is the beginning of a new phase for you, as a grant writer: accomplishing the task for which the money has been allocated.

When you have received the check, the first recommended step is to write a thank-you letter to the funder. Take a look at the sample on page 117.

Using Funds Ethically

When you receive a grant check, be sure to use the money for the specific uses for which funds were awarded. Foundations award the money in trust and expect recipients to honor that trust. For example, if you are an individual artist and won $10,000 to photograph a rare ape species in Indonesia, use the money for the purposes intended. Buying a new car or shopping is an unethical use of funds. You can also get into legal trouble if public grant funds are being used unethically.

Sample Thank-You Letter

Angelina Lambert
35 Memory Lane • New Orleans, Louisiana, 00000

August 15, 20xx

Mr. Kenneth Stephenson, Executive Director
World Heritage and Archive Foundation
New Orleans, Louisiana, 00000

Dear Mr. Stephenson,

Thank you for awarding me with a grant of $35,000 to conduct research in Greece. I will keep you updated on the progress of the project.

Sincerely yours,

Angelina Lambert

Angelina Lambert

Keep Receipts

It is the grant writer's responsibility to advise the organization staff to hold on to all receipts documenting how the grant money was spent. Sometimes foundations specifically ask for proof of expenses. Receipts give an indication of how monies were spent and whether the project was conducted at all. This is especially true in the case of grants for international projects. Receipts are usually requested from individual grant winners and, less frequently, from nonprofit organizations. Saving receipts also is helpful for tax purposes. In the event of an audit, you can prove how you spent the grant money.

Starting a Grant-Writing Business

Operating a homebased business can give you the best of both worlds. Like all small business owners, you enjoy the satisfaction of being your own boss and being the person who makes the decisions.

Becoming an Entrepreneur Is an Art, Not a Talent

The best grant writers think and act like entrepreneurs. The desire to become a grant writer or start your own grant-writing business requires an entrepreneurial spirit: motivation, willingness to learn, and a positive attitude. Becoming an entrepreneur is not a talent, but an art that can be learned.

> **Smart Tip** *Tip...*
>
> People are not born as entrepreneurs; rather life experiences shape them and spark their enterprising spirit into a flame.

Are You an Entrepreneur?

Successful entrepreneurs are multifaceted individuals. They have a lot of color in their lives. This section outlines some points to help determine whether you have what it takes to become an entrepreneur.

Entrepreneurs See Opportunities Where Others See Problems

This may be the factor that defines an entrepreneur. Entrepreneurs have dreams and visions. They have the ability to move forward amid obstacles to achieve goals. Challenges are like the wind on entrepreneurs' backs, constantly keeping them moving forward and not looking back. What others might see as a stumbling block, entrepreneurs see as a steppingstone.

Entrepreneurs are Hard Workers

Often, entrepreneurs enjoy the freedom to do what they like in life and work tirelessly to achieve that goal. They have the freedom to do what they love. However, being an entrepreneur is not necessarily an easy life either. It can mean working on a laptop tirelessly for long hours. As an entrepreneur however, you create your own opportunities and you create a work environment that reflects your values, not those of someone else.

> **Smart Tip** *Tip...*
>
> Entrepreneurs are usually self-made individuals who have tapped into their creativity, resources, and skills to provide a service or product that contributes to society.

Education Is Not a Requirement; Determination Is

Entrepreneurship is not limited by your abilities or education, but is propelled by determination and persistence. Some leading entrepreneurs did not complete high school, but they were driven to do what they love and did not fall by the wayside. To become a successful grant writer, you don't need a Ph.D., but you do need a desire to succeed. You must be willing to do what it takes to achieve your dreams and not settle for less.

It All Begins with an Idea

Success starts with an idea, new or repackaged. To be an entrepreneur, you don't have to come up with a new invention or product. You do have to provide a product or service that fills a consumer need. You can develop market knowledge by applying your creativity and intelligence.

Entrepreneurship is about connecting your business idea to the needs of your market. Entrepreneurs are constantly discovering new markets and trying to figure out how to supply those markets efficiently and make a profit. For example, if you are working for a nonprofit that takes on projects that sustain earth's natural resources, an innovative and eco-friendly idea to convert rainwater into bottled water can increase your chances of winning a grant.

Ability to Change with the Times

Entrepreneurs need to adapt to the needs of consumers and the changing economy. A lack of enthusiasm for change prevents many individuals and businesses from achieving their dreams.

20 Traits of an Entrepreneur

Entrepreneurs have dreams and visions. They cultivate character traits that help them to achieve those dreams and visions. Here are some of those personal attributes.

1. *A positive attitude.* No matter how many entrepreneurial characteristics you have or develop, they won't do any good unless you combine them with a positive attitude. Entrepreneurs are optimists—they have to see opportunities where others see problems.

2. *Motivation.* You must have the ability to motivate yourself and others.

Entrepreneurs have an inner force that continuously pushes them to accomplish goals. Time is an investment, not something to be wasted.

3. *Perseverance*. Refuse to quit, and have a willingness to keep goals in sight and work toward them, despite obstacles and rejections. Entrepreneurs don't give up easily.

4. *Ability to change with the times*. See change as an ally. Entrepreneurs realize that holding on to the good things of today and yesterday, and using them to move forward, is healthy.

5. *Confidence*. Believe that you can do what you set out to do, and don't settle for less. Entrepreneurs have inner confidence and can stay away from any traps that others may set to steer them away from their goals.

6. *Drive and stamina*. Entrepreneurs on a mission are like an engine that never stops. They are always moving, physically, emotionally, and spiritually.

7. *Honesty*. Maintain your commitment to tell the truth and deal with people fairly. Entrepreneurs establish credibility and earn the trust of people they are dealing with.

8. *Discipline*. Stay focused, and stick to schedules and deadlines. Entrepreneurs stay on course by not getting distracted by life's clutter.

9. *Ability to adapt*. Practice your ability to cope with new situations and find creative solutions to problems. Entrepreneurs are flexible and open to new ideas. They are willing to try something different.

10. *Competitive*. Entrepreneurs must be willing to compete with people who have achieved higher goals, thus striving for excellence—not mediocrity.

11. *Organized*. You must be able to bring structure your life, and keep your tasks and information in order. Entrepreneurs are constantly working on to-do lists.

12. *Persuasive*. Entrepreneurs have charisma and charm; they are able to convince people to see a particular point of view and get them interested in ideas.

13. *Risk-takers*. Entrepreneurs constantly feel challenged to do something different and have the courage to expose themselves to possible losses by treading unknown waters.

14. *Understanding*. Practice your ability to listen and empathize with other people.

15. *Dreams*. While others may ridicule, laugh, or try to dissuade, entrepreneurs silently nurture their dreams and constantly work to achieving them.

16. *Effective at time management*. You must be able to manage time wisely and efficiently. Time is valuable and often means money. Wasting time is an opportunity lost.

17. *Effective at stress management*. You must be able to manage stress well. Entrepreneurs have to oversee many facets of a business; there may be times

when funds are low. The ability to keep your head high during crunch time is key.

18. *Hardworking*. Hard work is at the core of success. Entrepreneurs must have a strong work ethic.

19. *Visionary*. Have a clear vision of your business and personal goals, and balance the two. Entrepreneurs have both a long-term and short-term vision. But this vision is not set in concrete. Be flexible to change direction as circumstances arise.

20. *Worthy of respect*. Respect is something that needs to be earned, not demanded. Most entrepreneurs value the respect of their clients. Don't become casual in your professional relationships or establish a higher level of authority.

Effective Salesmanship

At its core, entrepreneurship is about selling. Salesmanship skills are needed for two things:

1. To sell your grant-writing skills to a nonprofit, corporation, government, or individual

2. To persuade the funder to invest money in your project

Successful grant writers must become good at selling their services. A grant writer must overcome the fear of getting turned down by a funder. After all, it's only a "no."

Good salespeople create the need for their product or service. After introducing your grant-writing business to your prospect, create a need for his situation and your service. When you are meeting with a nonprofit, ask as many open-ended questions as you can to learn about the organization's experience with the funding request. This way, you find out about the organization's concerns rather than simply telling about how wonderful your service is. In the case of an interview with a funder, listen and provide answers to the funder's queries.

The 3-D Approach

To become a good salesperson, you must know your service. You must articulate what your business does and how it can help the customer. The 3-D approach helps prepare you for possible scenarios that you may encounter when making a sales call. By thinking through every possibility, you will be better prepared in determining how best to approach a client and handle objections.

Before making your sales pitch, get a sheet of paper and divide it into three columns. In the first column, write the benefits your service brings to society. In the second column, list the customer needs or problems that each benefit solves. In the third column, list the questions you will ask to determine if the problem or need exists. If you speak from a list of prepared questions, you will have more confidence in your sales pitch as a grant writer.

Successful salespeople are good listeners. This is an art that can be learned through training, correction, and practice.

People can always recognize a good listener. This trait is visible in facial expressions, the eyes, body gestures, and the types of questions raised within a conversation. People are often so concerned about what they are going to say next, they don't pay full attention when the other person talking. Be alert to verbal and nonverbal cues. Listen to the words and also the way they are said. Good presenting is intertwined with good listening.

Good salespeople stay open to others' perspectives and avoid making judgments. They ask open-ended questions and respect the perspectives expressed by clients. In addition, an effective grant writer uses silence frequently in interactions with others, allowing the speaker to express herself.

Being prepared for presentations and interviews is a trait that most successful salespeople share. You may have a great project idea that fits the funder's needs, but if you fumble in your presentation, the grant may slip through your fingers. Prepare in advance and practice your speech out loud in front of the mirror. People do judge you by the way you look, and first impressions can make or break a sale. Dress, gestures, speech, and demeanor are important.

Beware!

A funky hairstyle may work for high school, but it does not sit too well for an interview with a funder when you are requesting a grant. Professional grant writers dress professionally and practice good grooming. You need to look conservative and project the image of a successful person.

Salesmanship is a continuous process, and every prospect is different. After every sales call or presentation, whether a face-to-face meeting with a funder or submitting a federal grant application, think about the things that went right or wrong. What techniques did you use to persuade the funder to award a grant? How did you present your project idea? How did you get the corporate CEO to talk about his business needs? What are the the funder's needs that you should remember at your next meeting? Incorporate all the positive things that you did to your next presentation in order to improve your sales technique.

Start-Up Basics

Starting a business requires a lot of legwork: determining your plan for the business, obtaining funding, legalizing your business's structure, opening a bank account, and finding office space. While the requirements for these steps may vary, some standard rules apply.

Develop a Business Plan

The Small Business Association (SBA) defines a business plan as follows:

A business plan precisely defines your business, identifies your goals, and serves as your firm's resume. The basic components include a current and pro forma balance sheet, an income statement, and a cash flow analysis. It helps you allocate resources properly, handle unforeseen complications, and make good business decisions. Because it provides specific and organized information about your company and how you will repay borrowed money, a good business plan is a crucial part of any loan application. Additionally, it informs sales personnel, suppliers, and others about your operations and goals.

A business plan should be a living, breathing, ever-changing document. As the road map for your business, it will change constantly as you meet goals and set new ones. You will frequently review and update your business plan.

In addition, lenders may ask to see your business plan as they evaluate your loan request. It's important that you invest significant time developing and refining your plan *before* launching your business.

Start-Up Funding

The required start-up funding for a grant-writing business is low. Basically, you need a computer, office desk, and printer. If you want to set up an office space for the business, you will require more funds to cover rent, office furniture, communications systems, and staff. Once you have determined the amount of capital you need for the start-up phase of your grant-writing business, evaluate the potential sources of financing. It may be difficult for you to attract outside capital before you have established a track record.

Debt is a common source for funding new businesses. Debt financing can take many forms, but basically it means a lender has loaned you funds that you are obligated to repay in the future. Debt financing does not give the lender an ownership stake in the business; it is simply your promise to repay a loan.

Here are some common forms of debt financing:

- Your own resources: money from personal savings, family, and friends
- A bank loan
- The Small Business Administration (SBA)
- Leasing companies

Your Own Resources

This is the first place you should start, for many reasons. First, using your own funds is the least risky proposition from an asset-seizure point of view: You (the lender or investor) are not likely to foreclose on you (the borrower). Second, external lenders want to see that you have funds at risk.

Outside financing may be scarce in the beginning, and the more of your own money you have, the better the likelihood of financial stability and growth. You may have to save for a considerable amount of time to start your own business. However, it is important to remember that, just as you wouldn't invest all of your life's savings in a single stock, you shouldn't devote all of your money to your business. Make sure you have a number of saving vehicles for the future.

Bank Loan

A bank is the most common lending source for small businesses. Most businesses don't need a tremendous amount of outside financing to start or sustain the venture. In fact, many begin with less than $10,000 in working capital.

Here are some questions that bankers may ask as you apply for a loan.

- How much money do you want?
- What are you going to do with the money? (Be specific when you identify what the loan will be used for.)
- How will your company benefit by borrowing additional funds and taking additional risk?
- When will the loan be repaid? (If you plan to repay the loan within a short time — say, one year—then consider a single-payment loan. If you need to establish a cash flow from your business to make your loan payments, ask for a term loan, with payments spread out over several years.)
- How are you planning to repay the loan? (The person applying for the loan must

> **Smart Tip** *Tip...*
>
> Ultimately the person deciding on the loan is the banker. Sometimes there is a tendency to think that if everything looks good on a loan application form, that a loan will be approved. However, the banker is the ultimate deciding person in the process.

describe clearly how the loan will be paid off. It does not necessarily mean selling off your assets, but any way the loan can be repaid.)

- What are your contingency plans to repay the loan in case your business plan stalls? (You need to spell out how you will generate the funds necessary to repay the bank loan.)

Small Business Administration (SBA)

The SBA is a government agency set up to help small businesses succeed. A small-business loan can be the tool that nets you enough capital to create your dreams. Not only is this organization a great resource for finding capital, but the SBA also can provide the small-business owner with invaluable advice in getting started and seeking loans from other sources. Some of the loan programs offered through the SBA include:

- SBA low-documentation loans
- SBA microloans
- Other microloans programs

> **Beware!**
> Proceed with caution when borrowing start-up funding from friends, relatives, and in-laws. Some genuinely may want to help you with a little boost when you are first starting out. Others may be shrewd investors, wanting to make money by giving you a loan at a higher interest than the bank, knowing you have been denied by a financing institution. So, beware!

Leasing Companies

Leasing companies specialize in financing manufacturing or office equipment. You may find that the company that you purchase the equipment from has a leasing division and can handle the entire transaction for you. Equipment leases are always secured by the equipment being leased, so if you fall behind on your payments, you risk losing the equipment. On the other hand, the interest rates for this type of finance tend to be low because of the secured nature and because the company may be using the lease as a purchase incentive.

Business Structures

The three basic business organizational structures are:

1. Sole proprietorships
2. Partnerships
3. Corporations

Sole Proprietorship

Once you begin providing services with the intention of making money, you become a sole proprietor of a business. Your business expenses are tax-deductible, all income is taxable, and you assume the liabilities of the business. When you are the only one in charge of your business, you are the sole proprietor. You and your business are one.

A sole proprietorship is the most common and easiest type of business to create. Any one person who performs any services of any kind is, by default, a sole proprietor—unless the business has been set up otherwise. However, there aren't any restrictions on how big a sole proprietorship can become. It depends on the owner or proprietor.

In a sole proprietorship, all profits go directly to the owner. The disadvantage is that all legal and financial obligations incurred by the company also are passed directly to the owner. In a sole proprietorship, you are personally responsible for all the business's obligations, such as debt and financing.

Partnership

A partnership is formed whenever two or more people decide to enter a for-profit business venture. Typically, each partner owns a portion of the company's profits and debts, a structure that is set up in a written agreement between the parties. You do not need to file any special paperwork to form a partnership, but you should make sure you and your partner sign an agreement regarding each person's rights and liabilities.

When two or more people form a partnership, they are essentially married from a business standpoint. All liability is passed to the partners. There are two kinds of partnerships: limited and general. A limited partnership provides certain partners with a maximum financial liability equal to their investment. To maintain this limited financial liability status, these partners cannot participate in the daily operation of the business. The general partner is responsible for the day-to-day management of the business. Limited partners invest in the company and rely on the general partner to run the business.

Corporation

A corporation is a legal entity created through the state where the business is incorporated. A corporation is a separate and distinct business entity that is responsible for itself. Upon formation, the corporation issues shares of stock to shareholders, the owners. The percentage of ownership is based on the number of shares owned compared with the total number of shares sold. A board of directors elected by the shareholders manages the corporation. This board then appoints officers to handle the day-to-day affairs of the company. In essence, the board members represent the interests of the shareholders in the company operations.

Registering Your Business Name

The process of registering a business name differs by state, so check with your state or county government, chamber of commerce, or small-business development center. Typically there is a search for similar names before you register yours. Even after you register a business name, it is possible that another business out of state or in a different industry also will register and use the same name. But registration does give you some rights, especially in the face of a potential competitor using your business name or similar one. Find out how long your registration is valid and whether it needs to be renewed at any point. You don't want to go to all the trouble to register a name, build the business, and then lose the name to someone else five years down the road because you forgot to renew it.

Doing Business As (DBA)

The "Doing Business As" (DBA) form is sometimes called a fictitious name statement. A DBA gives you the rights to the name within the jurisdiction of the governing body, which is typically your county. If you want to call your grant-writing services "Gifted Hands Writing," you must file a DBA with the local authorities. This is usually done at the county clerk's office in the area where you plan to do your business.

Employer Identification Number (EIN)

If you plan to hire any employees or if you choose a form of business other than a sole proprietorship or have a retirement plan or need to withhold income tax, an EIN is a must. This is the equivalent of a social security number. In the same way that you personally have a taxpayer identification number (your Social Security number), an EIN identifies your business for tax purposes. To file for an EIN, use Form SS-4 issued by the IRS. Form SS-4 is available at post offices, public libraries, online, or by contacting the IRS.

If, on the other hand, you are a sole proprietorship without employees, you can simply use your Social Security number. Remember that as a sole proprietor, you are not an employee of the business.

Business Bank Accounts

Once you have registered your business name, you can head to the bank to open a business checking account. You could, of course, do this previously, but because you probably want your business name on your checks, you don't want to order checks until you are certain of the name.

Banks offer a wide array of services, often with an equally wide array of fees. Most home businesses can get along fine with a conventional checking account. (As a sole proprietor, the bank considers you and the business the same financial entity anyway.) A conventional account also is cheaper than a so-called business account, which can involve a monthly charge as well as charges for each deposit, each check written, and so forth. Check with your bank.

While you may not think you need a separate bank account for your business, you will be glad you do when it comes time to do your taxes. The IRS strongly recommends keeping all personal and business finances separate. This may be hard sometimes, but painstaking record-keeping is absolutely necessary if you are called upon to justify your business deductions.

> **Tip...**
>
> **Smart Tip**
> Drive thy business or it will drive thee.
> —Benjamin Franklin

A separate business account is seen as more professional by your vendors. A home business sometimes is not taken as seriously as a conventional business. Some of your clients may treat you casually when you write personal checks, knowing you have not drawn distinctions between your home life and your business life. Go the extra mile to show that even though you operate out of your home, you do things in a professional way.

Negotiating a Lease

Unless you are starting a homebased business (which we discuss next) or have enough cash upfront to buy an office space in your area, you likely will be leasing office space. A lease is a contract between you (i.e., the owner of the grant-writing business) and the landlord (i.e., the owner of the property). A lease establishes the terms of using a specific area of space for a certain length of time. The lease price is typically based on square footage.

Before signing a lease, look for wording that gives you flexibility and control. Avoid clauses that give power to the landlord and obligate you excessively. For example, your lease should include a statement that the space provided will be suitable for use as a professional writing service, addressing noise level, etc. This gives you a legal right to complain if the landlord fails to provide you with a quiet and professional environment.

Ensure the lease becomes void if the municipality refuses to approve zoning for a grant-writing business at that location. Otherwise you could be stuck with a lease on a space where you cannot operate your business.

You also may want to negotiate a lease that is renewable at your option. You don't know for sure that you will succeed in your business or that you will like the location. Give yourself the option to leave after six months or a year. Simultaneously give yourself the option to renew for a second and third year if your practice is successful.

Starting a Homebased Grant-Writing Business

Many successful grant writers establish profitable homebased businesses. Grant writing is now considered to be among the most attractive careers for those seeking increased personal income as well as flexible, autonomous, and meaningful work.

Starting and running a grant-writing business involves continuous learning. A lot of learning occurs from mistakes that you make along the way and vow never to repeat. Other learning comes from interactions with customers, fellow business owners, and friends who lead you toward success.

Qualities of a Successful Home Businessperson

Running a business from home might be just the right thing—for the right kind of person, at the right time of life, and for the right reasons. To get a sense if you are the right person, ask yourself these questions:

- Do you currently maintain a household budget and stick to it?
- Do you track household expenses monthly, project your needs, and save regularly for large purchases?

- Are you comfortable with change, unpredictability, and risk-taking?
- Do you enjoy the challenge of needing to reach a revenue goal each month, or does the thought make you tense and uncomfortable?
- Are you energized by the challenge of solving problems, or does encountering problem after problem leave you tired and discouraged?
- Are you a go-getter?
- Do you enjoy being on your own, not missing the company of co-workers?

Stat Fact
In April 2007, Spectrem, a Chicago-based research firm, found that overall, about 12 percent of American families own all or part of a privately-held business.

Good Reasons to Start a Homebased Grant-Writing Business

Working out of the home has become trendy. More and more people are doing it—and loving it. Is a homebased grant-writing business for you? There are many considerations to keep in mind when you are deciding whether it makes sense to operate your business from your home. Some of these considerations are financial, while others relate to the effects on your personal life.

It's not a good idea to start a business because you have had difficulty finding a full-time job that interests you or meets your financial goals. A business is more than a job; it is a serious commitment to your customers who rely on you. If you are currently employed and thinking about quitting to start a business, don't give up the stability of your day job until you can replace that income in the near future.

There are many good reasons to start a homebased business. This section lists some of them.

You Want a Change of Lifestyle

This is a common reason for starting home businesses and is a good one, as long as the lifestyle you seek involves hard work. Running a home business does not mean lounging around watching soap operas during the day. Rather, it means taking charge of your life, determining your own goals, and being responsible for your own achievements.

You Are Determined to Be Successful

The drive to succeed—and having a clear idea of what you mean by "succeed"—will be invaluable. You set goals and consistently work toward them. You will not settle for less.

You Have Ambition

This factor, by itself, is a good reason to start your own grant-writing business. People with ambition make life choices that keep them in a state of growth, not stagnant. Ambition is a good thing, provided it steers your life and decisions in a healthy direction.

Smart Tip — Tip...

A home business will certainly be challenging. You have to have self-discipline to motivate yourself. There isn't a clock to punch in your hours.

You Want to Be Your Own Boss

Many people who start their own businesses want to be their own boss. Most people are tired of being overworked or dealing with bosses who treat employees poorly. Being your own boss is a fine motivation, but success often means that the business, and the customers who come with it, are in fact your new bosses.

Running a homebased grant-writing business enables you to set your own hours. Some American companies are finding that employees are more productive when they are allowed to choose where and when they work. Companies are trying to get away from the 9-to-5 mentality and encouraging workers to set their own hours.

Free Day Care

Free day care is a possibility if the income from grant writing is sufficient to meet daily living expenses. However, in the early years of grant writing, all these perks, such as free day care and vacation, may not be affordable. When you are freelancing as a grant writer you can stay at home and take care of your children, while working at the same time. You can create an on-site child care system for yourself. A homebased grant writing business gives time off to bond with the kids. This is important not only for mothers, but for fathers also.

Stat Fact

According to a poll taken by MSN.com in April 2007, about 70 percent of employees at Best Buy's corporate headquarters in Minneapolis, Minnesota, set their own schedules, working enough at whatever location they like to meet certain agreed-upon performance objectives. Productivity has jumped 33 percent as a result.

More Vacation Time

A homebased grant-writing business offers more vacation time. As a freelancer, you can establish your vacation schedule. If you have had an exceptionally good year, maybe you can treat yourself to a month-long vacation. Since you are your own boss, you can decide the time of year you want to take your vacation. A vacation can do wonders for your work life as well as personal well-being.

Staying Motivated

Motivation is the foundation for any successful homebased grant-writing business. The first step to staying motivated is to understand what actually motivates you to begin with. The list of motivating factors can be varied. Examine your root causes for your desire to start a homebased business.

Stat Fact

The average number of vacation days is slowly edging up, rising from 10.9 annually in 2000 to 11.7 in 2006, according to Hewitt Associates. With health-care costs rising, many companies see increased vacation time as a good benefit in exchange for employees' paying higher medical costs.

- *A new beginning.* Did you start your business to start anew? Good for you. Life is about new beginnings. Give your life a fresh start.

- *Control.* Did you want to start a business because you wanted complete control over your work life?

- *Money.* Did you leave a job because you felt as if you were spending your time making someone else rich?

- *Creativity.* Did you feel your talents could be better used or better developed, or that your employer wasn't helping you expand your horizons?

- *An unhappy work environment.* Were you working for a dysfunctional boss who treated you poorly, which in turn, affected your self-confidence and cost your relationships with others?

Place your finger on what motivated you in the first place. Find ways to use that motivating factor or factors to reinvigorate your enthusiasm for your business on a daily or even hourly basis. Come up with motivating techniques that work for you.

Smart Tip

Tip...

Running your own grant-writing business may be tougher work than anything you have tried before, but it also offers rewards that are generally greater than what your current employer can give you. Change your job and change your life.

Addressing Common Fears

Fear prevents most people from achieving their dreams in life. Here are some common factors that affect the decision involved with starting a homebased grant-writing business:

Will My Family Support My Decision?

This may be the first question you need to answer. You are sure to encounter many more roadblocks in starting a business—and your spouse/partner can help or hinder you. In a healthy relationship, partners support each other's goals and want the other to be happy. Talk to your spouse. If he or she is opposed to your idea, see if there is a compromise.

What about Health Insurance?

Some people are afraid to start their own businesses because they don't think they can get health insurance. Believe it or not, you *can* get health insurance as a self-employed grant writer. It is possible that, depending on your personal circumstances, your coverage will cost more. But as a home business entrepreneur, you might be able to earn more than you do in your current job and it might be tax-deductible. Don't let the health care issues scare you off. Investigate insurance costs and build that expense into your business plan.

What about Retirement?

There are many people who give their entire lives to jobs they truly dislike, in order to ensure a safe retirement. Choosing a job you like is probably a good idea. Are you making yourself miserable today so you can be comfortable in 10, 20, or 30 years? Many people look back at their lives with regret, wondering what they could have done to lead more productive and career-healthy lives. Financial advisors can provide a wealth of information on individual retirement plans, investment vehicles such as stocks, bonds, and treasury bills, and how to make your money grow independently from an employer.

What about My Children's Education?

I've heard people say, "I need to keep working at my day job so my children can go to college." But, have you considered setting an example by driving yourself to excellence. Settling for mediocrity out of fear is not a healthy example to set. Your children also may have a lack of confidence and enthusiasm to excel in life. If you are afraid to take a risk, will your children hold back from trying to achieve their dreams?

The Homebased Business and Positive Self-Esteem

Self-esteem is a key ingredient to success. If you don't feel good about yourself, it rubs into your day-to-day affairs, family, and friends.

Maintaining positive self-esteem is an ongoing life challenge, regardless of where you work. In many ways, working in your own homebased business can be an uplifting experience. In other ways, you have to remember to pat yourself on the back, since you don't have a boss to do it for you.

Self-esteem is personal and needs to be addressed before you start feeling too negative. If you have friends who make you feel less than adequate because you are no longer the renowned guru for a well-known company, maybe you should spend less time with those people until you feel more accomplished. Most likely, your friends will be so impressed with your bravery in starting your own business that they offer their sincere praise.

Smart Tip

Cultivating positive self-esteem can help you carry out a profitable grant-writing business. People with positive self-esteem are productive, motivated, and goal-oriented. People with low self-esteem people are often unproductive and lack motivation.

People with high self-esteem have associations and friendships with others who strive to excel in life and not settle for less. They are always in a forward momentum, trying to better themselves. Associate with people who will serve as catalysts to help you get to a higher level, not lower your standards.

If you came from a "regular job," your self-esteem can suffer from losing an impressive job title beside your name. Or maybe your self-esteem depreciates on those trips to the bank when you are no longer depositing tidy sums of money in the form of regular paychecks but instead are withdrawing weekly sums for bare-bones living expenses.

Office Space

The traditional concept of "office space" is changing. With the internet, a successful grant-writing business can be run with just one piece of equipment: a laptop. Furthermore, a grant-writing business can be run from anywhere in the world, at any place, at any time. You can be at a coffee shop around the corner typing a proposal on your laptop, and that becomes your office space; you could be in a hotel in Russia e-mailing a proposal draft to a nonprofit agency in Hawaii. The majority of grant writers, however, establish a traditional, physical work space that they call their office.

Smart Tip

Most homebased business owners found the way of life and standard of living they wanted by setting goals and following a planned path to those goals. You also can follow that path and do what you like for a living.

A grant-writing business requires some level of office space from which you can make phone calls, create invoices, and do your day-to-day bookkeeping. If all your work is done via phone, mail, fax, or computer, then your options are much simpler, as you don't need the paraphernalia associated with a traditional office.

Office needs vary based on the type of services you provide. A grant writer working full time for a nonprofit may be given a cube or a room, whereas a grants consultant traveling the country may rely on the laptop as the main piece of office "space." A grant-writing business, especially one that attracts clients to the site, needs to have a traditional office.

> **Smart Tip**
>
> Most businesses require high start-up capital. A homebased grant-writing business on the other hand, requires very little. A computer with basic programs and the ability to surf the web are sufficient to get you started.

A Room of Your Own

The first step is to claim a work space big enough to call your own. The place and size of your work space differs. If you are renting a 7-by-10-foot room in a three-bedroom house, then your workspace may be your bed for a while. If you have a larger home, the space can be a small desk plus a file cabinet.

Here are some considerations for establishing at-home work space. If you don't have a separate room for your office, you need to get a little more creative. You will be amazed at where you can carve out a defined office space. Do some detective work around the house, looking for areas that could give up a few square yards to convert to private office space without requiring a huge renovation. The most successful business owners, homebased or not, make do for the time being and plan for changes upon reaching certain stages of financial success.

 Beware!

Don't let the physical size of an office limit you from claiming a place to work. For some, the office may be the garage or a coffee shop around the corner. Lack of office space should not be a factor to dissuade you from starting your own grant-writing business. It is not the size of the office that matters, but your passion for getting started.

Basements often hide useable space, but be mindful of dampness or flooding problems. With a little basic carpentry to make a partition, some damp-proofing paint on the walls, and a couple of hundred dollars of professional electrical work, you might be able to create a nice work space. The laundry room is another area that can be transformed into an office space. If you start with one of these "almost-ideal" office locations, consider setting aside a little savings marked specifically for a renovation to create a more workable office space, especially if your business grows with any speed.

A separate room with a door that shuts is the ideal home-office space. This allows you to better define that fine line between your personal life and your work life, which is perhaps the biggest challenge for homebased business owners. Not only can you shut the door and walk away at the end of the day, but you can better tune out those after-hour work calls that, if you hear the phone ring, you may be tempted to answer. The "out of sight, out of mind" adage certainly works here.

There are several advantages to separating your business from your personal life:

- A distinct definition of work space and personal space can have a positive psychological effect on your productivity.
- A closed door is better protection against your baby accidentally spilling fruit juice all over your need statement.
- Your family won't have to listen to all your business phone conversations.
- Your clients won't hear _The Terminator_ reruns playing on the television in the background

Office Furniture

If you can afford top-of-the-line office furniture, go for it. But if you can't, not to worry. A couple of Saturday mornings at yard sales may yield reasonably priced office furniture. If yard sales aren't your idea of fun, check the Yellow Pages or the newspaper for places that sell used office equipment. Another place to visit is the landfill. Some

Office Essentials

Essentials for your office include:

- ○ About 30 hanging folders
- ○ File-folder labels
- ○ A bulletin board and pushpins
- ○ Your organization's letterhead (first and second pages) and envelopes
- ○ A bookcase or shelf to store research materials
- ○ A telephone with long distance access
- ○ A computer and printer
- ○ Access to a photocopier

have a separate section for furniture, where you can pick up items for a small fee.

Desk Location

Choosing a place for your desk is important as you will spend most of your time writing there. Consider the location of your desk carefully. A private or secluded spot is desirable so you can work without interruption.

Whatever you choose for a desk, be sure it is computer friendly. Remember, as a grant writer, you will be spending a lot of time with this piece of furniture.

Chair

You will need a comfortable office chair. Office-supply stores keep many on hand. Sit in them all, and slide them up to one of the display desks. Buy a high-quality chair; it affects your posture and your back.

Bookshelves

You need at least one bookshelf in your office. Grant directories tend to be rather large and require shelving space. Bookshelves range from the most basic pressboard styles to those that are more like elegant showpieces. You also can use milk crates as temporary shelving space.

File Cabinets

A basic filing cabinet helps you to organize your files methodically. Consider what kind of documents you will be storing and choose either a legal- or letter-size cabinet.

Home-Office Technology

The right home-office technology is critical to staying connected. Technology is always in a state of flux. Staying informed of cutting-edge technology can save you time, resources, and energy. This section lists some of the essentials in office technology you may want to have.

Telephone

While your home phone might suffice during start-up, you quickly will see the need for a second line dedicated to your business. Most quality phones come with ring volume control. Better yet, find a model that allows you to shut the ringer off.

Many phones now come equipped for caller ID, which can be handy if you are trying to concentrate on a job and want to screen your calls. When you sign up for the service with your local phone company, at a monthly fee, the home of the caller and his number flash on the phone's LCD screen.

If you think you might need two business lines in the near future, two-line phones are readily available in a reasonable price range.

You may want to consider a cordless phone. That way if you need to be in another area of the house, you won't miss any calls or have to run to answer the phone. A speakerphone feature on the handset will be equally useful.

There are key differences in telephone technology. Analog phones are inexpensive, but have the shortest range and are easy to listen in on. Digital or Digital Spread Spectrum (DSS) phones cost more, but provide greater range and more security from eavesdropping.

If you spend a lot of time in your car, a cell phone is a must allowing you to call from the road to confirm or reschedule appointments, or to check directions. Cell phone plans vary. Call your local dealer or visit a retail outlet to get an idea of the monthly calling plan that best suits your business needs.

Answering Machines

An answering machine comes standard in many business-type phones. Don't have a cute message with music in the background. Have a basic message such as "You have reached Gifted Hands Writing. Thank you for contacting us. Please leave a message. For further information, you may visit our web site at www.giftedhandswriting.com."

Computer

The computer is practically solely responsible for the boom in home businesses. Before purchasing one, it is important to assess how you will use it. Here are some things to think about:

- Will your computer serve solely as a device to generate written proposals? Or will you need to work with graphics and spreadsheets?
- Will your grant-writing business rely on the construction of a large, complex mailing list?
- Will you use the computer for accounting, bookkeeping, tax calculations, and other functions?
- Will you want to be able to perform tasks with several files and programs running at one time?

Tip...

Smart Tip

Some nonprofits may be replacing their computers that are in good condition. You might be able to get a pre-owned machine for free or for a discount rate.

Laptop

Laptops are desirable for their portability. Some computer manufacturers offer docking stations that make it possible to use your laptop with a standard monitor and keyboard when you are at home. If you are on the road a lot, a laptop probably is the way to go.

Computer Accessories

You will need a printer. The ability to print in color is worthwhile and becoming almost standard with inkjet printers. If you will be printing a considerable amount, you may consider laser printers. They are fast and offer high-quality output. Printer speed is discussed in pages per minute (ppm), and obviously, the higher the number, the faster the printer.

If you are scanning photographs and doing a lot of graphics, a scanner will be useful. Be sure the scanner is compatible with your computer and software.

External hard drives, CDs, and USBs are common ways of storing information.

Photocopier and Fax Machine

A photocopier can be convenient to have in your home office. A copier may be especially handy if you are submitting federal applications, which may consist of thousands of pages.

Having a fax machine is handy, especially to provide additional materials as requested by funders. Some funders even accept faxed applications.

Internet Service

There is a monthly charge for internet service. You may need to choose between dial up, DSL, and cable. Local providers often also offer web site development as part of the package, a good thing if you plan to have a web site for your grant writing business. The rates for internet service vary; inquire with your local communications services.

Create a Systematic Filing System

Create a systematic filing system right from the start. Your applications, research information, and organizational documents can be filed in hard copy or on the computer. Some may opt to do both. If you are storing hard copies, manila folders are inexpensive and can help you to get organized. If you're filing electronically, you may use CDs, the hard drive, USB drive, or disks. Whichever filing method you choose, organize your files in a way that suits your grant-writing needs.

This section lists some types of files to create.

Organization and Program Files

You can't do a good job of grant seeking without knowing your client and its programs well. Once you gain this knowledge, you will refer to it again and again. In your "Organization and Program Files" area, create file folders with the following labels:

- Organization resume
- Board list
- Bios of key people
- Most recent 990-PF form
- 501(c)(3) letter
- Organization budget for current year
- Current financial statement
- Last two audited financial statements
- Bylaws
- Antidiscrimination policy
- Drug policy
- Newspaper clippings
- Letters of support

Community Files

An essential part of successful grant seeking is understanding and expressing the need that your community—be it your neighborhood, town, state, or country—has for the services your organization provides. You will be creating and maintaining a small library to document this subject.

In your "Community Files" area, create file folders with the following labels:

- Press clippings
- Anecdotes
- Statistics
- Published reports
- Newsletters and materials from other nonprofits

Funder Files

You will collect and process a great deal of information about the funders that award grants. You need to understand and organize this information to keep it accessible. Create one file folder for each funder you research or work with; file in your "Funder Files" area. Each funder file contains all your information about and correspondence with that funder. For example, if you are representing an organization that is applying for a grant from the United States Institute of Peace (USIP), create a separate folder for USIP. File the guidelines, newsletters, and applications in that folder.

Marketing Tips for Less Than $100

The reality for every grant writer is this: you *are* your business. It is up to you to market your grant-writing services in order to make a profit from your talent, hard work, and expertise.

Your marketing plan should identify your target market. Marketing efforts come in two types of packages: paid vs. unpaid. Paid promotion is usually some sort of advertising that you pay to run on a planned schedule. Unpaid promotion is publicity, such as word of mouth or referrals. The advantage of paid promotion is that it is predictable. With unpaid promotion you are often at the mercy of other people and their moods. However, unpaid promotion carries more credibility than any sales pitch.

Smart Tip

Plan your work and work your plan. Jumping haphazardly from one sales effort to the next is not the best way to sell your grant-writing skills. You need to create a plan that helps you identify your target market, prioritize your leads, and track your success.

Presentation is everything when it comes to marketing. Whether you are developing a brochure, an ad, or a newsletter, your marketing materials send a strong message about your grant-writing business. Materials should be well-written, attractive, and professional.

Bright Idea

Pursuing the right marketing strategies is critical to the financial success of your career as a grant writer. By using a carefully crafted combination of paid and unpaid promotions, just about any business can get its message out. With some basic market research, you can get that message to the people who matter, your target customers.

The tips in this section provide some business ideas that you can mold into your marketing plan. All of them might not work for your grant-writing business; select the ones to suit your specific needs. Tips are intended to help grant writers establish visibility, credibility, and enhance marketability.

Each tip costs less than $100 (although bear in mind that the same service can cost you more than $1,000). Some tips don't cost you a penny; rather, they require time, energy, and a positive attitude. Remember: The following steps need to be followed systematically and consistently over time. Don't expect overnight results.

Newsletters

Start a newsletter to promote your grant-writing business. Target nonprofits as your primary clients. By regularly sending out a quality newsletter, you can keep current clients, potential clients, the media, and other important sources updated about your business.

Here are some points to address in your newsletter:

- Information about what is unique about your grant-writing business.

- The services you are proud of. Mention any grant awards you have won recently; include their amounts.

- Include testimonials by nonprofit staff members who have hired you.

- Encourage readers to send you e-mail. Always remember to type in your e-mail address (e.g., e-mail us at info@giftedhandswriting.com) and include an automatic link (e.g., "Click Here to send an e-mail") Some computers can't open an e-mail automatically, so the address has to be manually typed in.

- Include a "Safe Unsubscribe" feature.

- Provide a list of URLs where readers can find more information.

- Once you have a newsletter, carefully cultivate a mailing list. Keep it in good shape and work to expand it.

Smart Tip

Tip...

Newsletters are one of the least expensive and most effective public relations tools that exist for drawing attention to your business. This is especially true with e-newsletters. Constant Contact is an excellent e-mail marketing tool for creating newsletters. Visit www.constant contact.com.

Press Releases

You can write a press release about nearly anything newsworthy that is related to your grant-writing business. Some topics include requests for proposals issued by a

---

Subscription Help

Subscriptions to grant-writing magazines help you keep in touch with the latest trends in the world of philanthropy. Some, especially magazines, are free online while others have a fee. If you are unsure about subscribing for a whole year, ask for a sample copy first. Some grant-writing related magazines and newsletters include *The Writer*, *The Foundation Newsletter*, *The Grants Advisor*, and *Corporate Philanthropy Reports*.

federal agency, reduced hourly writing rates for individual artists, or an upcoming grant-writing seminar. Some magazines, newspapers, and public radio stations promote press releases for free. Find out if this is an option in your area.

Philanthropic Activities

Giving is not just good for the soul, it's also good for business. Offer to volunteer your grant-writing services at a local nonprofit. For example, volunteer as a grant writer at the local fire department and help buy new fire trucks. This can earn you big points in the field of philanthropy.

Cultivate Referrals

People inevitably listen to a personal recommendation over a sales pitch. Word of mouth is a strong means of promoting your grant-writing business. Referrals are among the most profitable fruits of marketing. A referral from a present customer is stronger than an ad in the local paper.

In order to get quality referrals, it is important to have frequent contact with your clients. Simply ask your present customers for a referral. You also may have business-sized cards printed that say "Refer a nonprofit." For every referral that comes, offer your current client a discount or thank-you gift.

The Yellow Pages

The Yellow Pages are a powerful way to acquire new customers. Ad categories may vary with each directory. Place an ad in the writing, fundraising, or nonprofit section.

Create a Web Site

If you are a freelancer, create a web site to promote your grant-writing business.

Be sure your web address is printed on your business cards, brochures, and all other business-related materials. The more easily customers can find your web address, the more likely they are to visit your site. Offline marketing is as important as online marketing.

Print Ads

Print ads are one of the most powerful and popular methods of advertising. To be successful, maintain consistency. Keep the same image

Tip...

Smart Tip
Don't be misled by people who say it costs thousands of dollars to create a web site. Sure, it can. But you can create your own web site by following some basic instructions. Read books and articles online. There are also software programs that have simplified the process for beginners.

▲

and layout throughout your ad campaign. An advertisement should be easy to read, be easy to understand, and stand out when readers flip through a publication.

Business Cards

A business card can be a powerful promotion tool. Ideally a business card should include your name, company name, physical address, phone numbers, e-mail and web site addresses, and a brief description of what you do.

Think of your business card as a mini advertisement. Your aim is to get people who see it to contact you for a service. Create custom, full-color designs that connect you with your target market. Use quality paper, make the card easy to read, and keep it simple. Leave enough white space, and don't clutter your card with too much information.

Direct Mail

One of the most common methods to reach your target market is by direct mail. Mailing list companies have become more and more sophisticated in targeting certain demographic and niche groups. If you're smart about renting and managing mailing lists, you can get a lot for your money with a direct mail campaign. The list broker often can help design your direct mail piece and arrange for printing and mailing.

Do the research a marketing plan requires so that you know who your customers are. Then test the mailing lists that you think include those potential customers.

Working as a
Grant Writer

Grant writers perform an essential role for many charitable institutions, think tanks, colleges, universities, individuals, and other organizations seeking funds. As grant monies from the federal government, private philanthropic foundations, corporate foundations and individuals become more plentiful, the demand for highly skilled grant writers increases.

Career Opportunities in Grant Writing

Diversifying your earning potential as a grant writer is key to making profits. Create a healthy mix of income earning strategies. A grant writer can earn an income in several ways:

- *Writing grant proposals.* Individuals, non-profits, and government agencies hire grant writers to get money for various projects.

Stat Fact
According to Entrepreneur .com, grant consulting is the 12th most-thriving consulting business.

- *Organizing seminars and workshops.* Once you become established as a grant writer, you can organize seminars and work-shops on how to win grants.

- *Fundraising for nonprofits.* One of the tasks of the fundraiser is grant writing.

- *Publishing articles and books on how to win grants.* Trade journals and consumer magazines may look for articles on grants.

- *Developing a database of funding resources.* Searching and developing a list of potential funding resources that match your client's missions, goals, and activities.

- *Reviewing grant proposals.* A professional review of completed proposals before submission helps the submitting organization ensure the proposal is complete and fits the funder's guidelines. Tasks include proofreading, identifying weak-nesses, and revising the proposal accordingly.

- *Getting accredited to certify new grant writers.* Increasingly, organizations are seeking grant writers who are certified to pursue the profession. Being able to accredit individuals can get you a steady flow of income.

Some of the organizations that hire grant writers are:

- Animal-rights organizations
- Arts councils
- Churches
- Colleges and universities
- Community-based organizations
- Community developers
- Environmental groups
- Faith-based organizations
- Fire departments
- Government agencies

Beware!
Sometimes individ-uals apply for grants. For the most part, how-ever, individuals are not the best market for your business. Individuals often lack the money to pay a professional grant writer.

- Health care agencies
- Hospitals
- International nonprofits or NGOs (non-governmental organizations)
- Law-enforcement agencies
- Performing arts organizations
- Private and corporate foundations
- Public and private elementary/secondary schools
- Youth organizations

> **Tip...**
>
> **Smart Tip**
> Beginning grant writers normally charge $25 per hour or volunteer their services to gain experience in writing grant proposals. When you consider that in just a few short weeks you can be well on the way to establishing a successful career in grant writing, getting qualified as a grant writer is an excellent value and investment in your future.

Getting Qualified as a Grant Writer

Online learning offers a convenient opportunity for working adults to make a career change while keeping regular hours at their current jobs. Online courses about grant writing are usually ten weeks long. Here is a sample outline of an online grant-writing course:

Ten-Module Course Outline
1. Grant Writing I—Basic
2. Prospect Research
3. Proposal Budgeting
4. Grant Writing II—Intermediate
5. Collaboration and Partnerships
6. Evaluation Tools and Processes
7. Grant Writing III—Advanced
8. Business Planning
9. Getting Clients, Fees, and Contracts
10. Other Services for Earned Income as a Grant Writer

Attending grant-writing workshops and seminars is another way to get qualified. Grant-making organizations and individual grant writers present seminars and workshops in different parts of the country. Attending a few workshops can provide you with the necessary foundation to get started.

If you don't yet have adequate experience as a professional grant writer, consider volunteering at a local nonprofit. Virtually every nonprofit has a need for a grant writer. Volunteering your grant-writing services is an offer very few nonprofits would

Don't Give It Away

Volunteering at a local nonprofit to write grant proposals is one way of getting qualified. However, don't become a professional volunteer. People will gladly accept your professional services for free. But at some time you will have to say, "Enough with the compliments; show me the money." Very few professional grant writers "donate" their services beyond a few cherished projects, since grant writers depend on nonprofits for their careers.

refuse. By working for free, you can gain the experience and expertise needed to get a paying job. Choose a field that you have a passion for. For example, if you believe strongly in helping educate people in India about AIDS, then help to raise money for an international development agency working in that area.

Getting qualified as a generalist or specialist is another way to become a skilled grant writer. Medical grant writers, for instance, write for hospitals, medical researchers, clinics, universities, and other health-related organizations. Some grant writers specialize in educational grants for schools or colleges. Others focus on issues such as child abuse and neglect, or scientific research grants. Yet others prefer to write only one type of grant, perhaps for federal funding.

Once you are qualified, list your services on online sources. There are grant-writing associations that connect applicants with professional writers. Nonprofits also use referrals from major agencies such as the United Way, Red Cross, and UNICEF. Some of these larger organizations' databases may have a list of talented grant writers. Such databases may be a free service available to local nonprofits. Getting registered in such a database helps you network.

Getting Started as a Freelancer

Smart Tip

Unless you are an expert, you may not have the skills needed to write proposals for professionals in the fields of science, medicine, technology, or engineering. Their proposals will be read by peers in these highly specialized professions.

Freelancing is one of the most common ways for grant writers to get started. Grant writers can freelance for nonprofits, individuals, corporations, and a variety of other sources. To get your start as a grant writer, you need to first identify potential client organizations. Remember, large organizations employing full-time grant writers may seek contractual grant writers as the need arises. Develop contacts within these organizations and begin to network. Networking is key.

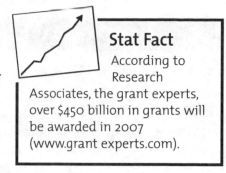
Contact the development officers of some of the nonprofit organizations near you. Regardless of if they employ grant writers as full-time staff members, ask to speak to the development officer to inquire about the organizations's need for grant writers on a consulting basis. There are a number of smaller nonprofit organizations that cannot afford full-time employees but hire grant writers on a part-time or special project basis.

Where to Look for Grant-Writing Jobs

Knowing where to look for grant-writing jobs is important. This section lists some places to get started.

Classifieds

Almost every major city newspaper and employment web sites advertise grant-writing jobs virtually every day. Grant-writing jobs may be indexed under "foundation," "grant-making," "philanthropy," "volunteerism," or "writing." In addition, grants newsletters, subscription databases, and publications (see Chapter 4) are excellent places to look for grant writing jobs. If you are applying for the job title of fundraiser, remember that it encompasses more than grant writing.

There are many types of classified ads. Take a look at the sample on page 152.

Foundation News and Commentary

Published by the Council on Foundations, this web site (www.foundationnews.org) features a job bank that lists hundreds of job sources every month. The sample ad on page 153 is one type of ad.

The Chronicle of Philanthropy

At www. philanthropy.com, many types of jobs are advertised under the following categories: fundraising, executive, program, and administrative. Jobs for grant writers are "fundraising," which includes alumni affairs, annual fund, capital campaigns, corporate relations and foundation relations, direct marketing, donor relations, fundraising administration, grant writing, major gifts, membership, planned giving, prospect research, special events, and other fundraising. There is a sample of this type of job listing on page 154.

▲

Sample Classified Ad

Job Title: Rose Foundation seeks a grant writer, full-time position

We currently have an opening for the position of Grant Writer. The Grant Writer will join a dynamic team of staff and board leaders dedicated to inspiring the most diverse population of youth in Boston. This full-time position will split his/her time between each organization, reporting to the Development Director. Successful candidates will evidence commitment to mission-driven organizations and have 3+ years grant writing experience.

Responsibilities will include:

- Acquiring and maintaining sound knowledge and understanding of each organization's mission, programs, target population, and strategic vision. Using this information to better prepare grants and guide the research process.
- Researching grant-making organizations and programs.
- Compiling, writing and editing all grant applications, exhibiting strong expository writing skills and excellent attention to detail.
- Preparing individual grant proposals in accordance with each grant-making organization's guidelines.
- Conducting follow-up communications with grant making organizations during their review processes in order to supply additional supportive material.
- Preparing and submitting all quarterly and/or annual reports, as required by each grant-making organization for each funded program.
- Responsibility for the creation of each organization's quarterly newsletter, including: writing, managing the editing process with a graphic designer, and printing and mailing processes with selected vendors.

E-mail resume and cover letter in confidence to
grantwriter@grantwriter.com

Sample Job Bank Ad

A private foundation is seeking a grants manager:

Location: Boston, Massachusetts

Posted by: The Education Center of Massachusetts

Job category: Fundraising & development, Grants administration

Salary: Competitive

Type: Full time

Language(s): English

Job posted on: May 20, 20xx

Area of focus: Children and Youth, Foundations, Fundraising, and Philanthropy

Qualifications:
Successful candidates should demonstrate:
- Appreciation, ability to convey vision and commitment to each organization's mission
- Three + years of grant writing experience
- Knowledge of the grant application process and the writing of applications
- Superior writing, speaking, and listening skills
- Success in planning, prioritizing, and coordinating multiple projects
- Excellent organizational skills
- Ability to research available grant opportunities
- Ability to gather, analyze, and evaluate a variety of data
- Ability to participate as a team player to coordinate grant projects
- Ability to work under pressure to meet deadlines for grant opportunities

Sample Chronicle of Philanthropy Job Listing

Position: Development Associate

Location: Virginia

Date posted: 5/12/20xx

A public interest law firm seeks an energetic, professional person to fill the role of Development Associate in this dynamic, fun, and growing organization. The ideal candidate will have a bachelor's degree and/or three years of experience. The position offers tremendous potential for growth and the opportunity to be part of a dynamic development team as it raises the Institute's $8 million annual budget. Specific responsibilities include drafting foundation reports and proposals and identifying new foundations. Must have strong writing skills. This job offers a competitive salary, full health, dental, and life insurance benefits, and a pension plan. Please send cover letter, resume, and writing sample.

The Grantsmanship Center

The web version of the *Grantsmanship Center* magazine's (www.tgci.com) has a link titled "Income opportunities," which lists job openings, social entrepreneurs, and fundraising jobs. Here is a sample classified ad taken from the Grantsmanship Center's web site.

Sample Grantsmanship Center Ad

Job Description of Development Officer and Fundraiser

Summary: Develops grants and marketing materials, and conducts research for funding sources in government, foundations, and corporations.

Responsibilities
- Develop grants from requests for proposals and renewals for corporations, foundations, and government agencies.
- Conduct research on potential funders including governmental agencies.

Sample Grantsmanship Center Ad, continued

- Write correspondence to corporations and foundations.
- Ensure that reports are submitted to funding sources and maintain copies.
- Responsible for annual appeal and assisting with other fundraising events.
- Be active participant in professional groups.
- Collect material for and write agency newsletter.
- Collect evaluation data on the delivery and quality of services from key programs.
- Respond to requests for specific information from external agencies.
- Answer information requests from the web site.
- Provide support to the CEO.
- Display the highest ethical and professional behavior and standards when working with students, parents, school personnel, and agencies associated with the school.
- Maintain positive, cooperative, and mutually supportive relationships with the central administration, parents, and representatives of resource agencies within the community.
- Other duties as assigned.

Requirements

Qualifications

- A minimum of a Bachelor's Degree in Social Work, Education, or related field.
- A minimum of three years successful grant-writing with government and other funding.
- Two years experience working in non-profit organizations.
- Excellent interpersonal and organizational skills.
- Excellent writing and speaking, skills.
- Experience working with or knowledge of inner city and Latino youth.

▲

Commission-Based Grants

Most grant writers require hourly or per diem compensation, rather than accept deferred payment contingent on grants received. This practice is often used by cash-strapped nonprofit organizations with little operational funds, but commission-based grants raise a number of ethical questions in the industry. For example, funders generally require that every expense be accounted for on a line-item basis. This means the application's budget must include a line for grant writing. However, grants are often requested to offset project costs—not to pay operational expenses such as grant writing. Funders don't like their money being used for commissions. Therefore, by including a grant-writing fee in the proposed budget, the grant application is put at risk of not being accepted.

> *Tip...*
>
> ## Smart Tip
> Never accept a grant-writing assignment for a percentage of the final grant award. First, you will not be paid unless the funding is awarded, and second, a financial stipend for grant writers is rarely, if ever, allowed under the terms of the grant-award agreement.

As a grant writer, you also will be taking a lot of risks when you tie your compensation with the success of the grant application. If the grant application is rejected, you have basically given your services for free. The success or failure of a grant application is not always contingent on the quality of writing of the grant proposal. Even if a grant writer submits an exceptionally persuasive grant proposal, there is always the likelihood of a funder rejecting it. Sometimes, grant applications are rejected because of poor timing, poor presentation by the applicant, or another reason beyond the

Stick to the Code

Some grant writers consider commission-based writing as highly unethical. Grant writers are paid a fee if the applicant wins a grant. This can be a risky proposition. In fact, the Code of Ethical Principles and Standards of Professional Practice of the National Society of Fund Raising Executives opposes deferred payment: "Members shall work for a salary or fee, not percentage-based compensation or a commission. Members shall not pay, seek, or accept finder's fees, commissions, or percentage compensation based on charitable contributions raised, and shall, to the best of their ability, discourage their organizations from making such payments based on charitable contributions."

grant writer's control. Grant writers should be given fair payment for work done on a grant application, regardless of if the grant funding is secured.

Commission-based grants also raise the question of how the grant writer will receive payment if the grant is paid out over a number of months or years. Say, for example, a grant of $800,000 is to be paid on a quarterly basis for four years. Will the grant writer be paid the commission as soon as the grant is approved, regardless of the actual fund disbursement? Or will the payment be made in sync with the grant's payment schedule?

Taking Your Grant-Writing Career to the Next Stop

There are other opportunities available to you once you have established yourself as a grant writer. Here are some of them.

Offer Grant-Writing Workshops or Courses

Once you become established as a grant writer, you can take your career to the next level by offering workshops in different parts of the country. You can get paid anywhere from $400 to $2,000 for a single workshop. Some of the workshops can be offered online, similar to online degrees.

Offering grant-writing workshops can be a profitable means of earning an income. In order to host workshops, you need to be qualified as a grant writer and have established a reputation as a professional in the field. Having a book published on grant writing is an advantage. Select a location where there are many nonprofits or aspiring grant writers who will attend the seminar. Rent a hotel conference center for eight hours (or less) and advertise online, in newspapers, and to nonprofits about the event. Set a registration fee that participants can pay online.

Another option is to offer grant-writing training courses in proposal writing and program development, grant administration, grant consulting, grant evaluation, and grant reviewing. Post curriculums online so applicants can pick the courses they want to sign up for.

Sample Grant-Writing Course Outline

Here is a sample outline that you can use for a grant writing workshop. It is from Gifted Hands Writing, a writing company that provides grant-writing services to individuals and organizations.

Sample Grant-Writing Course Outline

Gifted Hands Writing offers an online grant-writing course for people interested in grant writing as a career or those who just want to brush up on their grant-writing skills. The cost of the grant-writing course is $500 per module. Modules teach the basics of grant writing up through complicated grant proposals that require extensive research to describe the need for the project. Included in the course are research strategies to find hundreds of grant-funding opportunities and prospects in the participant's field of interest. At the end of the self-paced course, individuals will have the skills necessary to begin their own grant-writing career, whether it be a homebased business or as a professional grant writer for a nonprofit organization. Course descriptions include:

Introduction to Grant Writing

This detailed one-day workshop introduces beginning grant writers to the field of grant writing. Participants learn how to:

- Identify government, private, and corporate grant-funding sources
- Conduct a community needs assessment
- Write convincing problem statements
- Develop innovative program designs
- Create program-driven budgets
- Prepare grant proposals and applications
- Publish articles on how to win grants
- Write persuasive grant proposals
- Apply to government, private, and corporate grant programs
- Analyze grant applications and RFPs (request for proposals)
- Conduct a thorough needs assessment
- Develop innovative program activities
- Establish goals and objectives
- Disseminate information and program findings
- Plan for program sustainability
- Build strong budgets that withstand cuts
- Use writing styles for visual appeal
- Understand e-grant applications and online forms

Sample Grant-Writing Course Outline, continued

- Learn what happens after the grant is submitted
- Learn how federal grants are rated

Becoming a Certified Grants Reviewer

Learn the essentials of grant reviewing and how to become a professional reviewer. Topics include:

- Working with review panels
- Analyzing government, private, and corporate applications
- Critiquing proposals for strengths and weaknesses
- Building an internal grants-review team
- Becoming a grants reviewer for pay
- Understanding rules and guidelines for reviewers
- Scoring and ranking grant proposals
- Abiding by ethical standards

Becoming a Certified Grants Administrator

This course takes the grants administrator from the time the grant is announced to the close of the program. Topics include:

- Acquiring grant funds
- Preparing for a program and financial audit
- Using consultants and other contract services
- Planning for an on-site visit with program officers
- Working with external evaluators
- Evaluating program components
- Monitoring and amending your program budget
- Planning for program sustainability
- Applying effective administrative strategies
- Learning successful writing techniques
- Reviewing grant proposals and concept papers

Becoming a Certified Grants Consultant

Participants learn how to:

- Respond to funding notifications to avoid budget cuts

Sample Grant-Writing Course Outline, continued

- Conduct a market and competition analysis
- Develop a strategic business plan
- Set up legal and financial structures
- Diversify income streams—from presenting workshops to writing books
- Market services to build clientele
- Assess an RFP (request for proposal) for grant writers
- Negotiate fees and assemble pricing schedules
- Bid services to compete with other vendors
- Abide by ethical business standards
- Make a healthy profit from a grant-writing business
- Market a grant-writing business

Introduction to Evaluation

This course helps you to identify and work with an evaluator, write grant evaluations, and conduct an evaluation independently. Topics include:

- Learning interviewing methods
- Understanding the purpose of program evaluation
- Analyzing, interpreting, and reporting data
- Using evaluation data to improve program performance
- Designing effective evaluation plans
- Focusing the evaluation
- Establishing evaluation methods and tools
- Creating data collection models
- Developing surveys to measure program performance
- Applying the logic model to program components
- Using evaluation results for program improvement
- Abiding by standard ethics and guiding principles

Becoming a Foundation and Corporate Grants Specialist

Learn the tips for working with foundations and corporations. Topics include:

- Writing convincing grant proposals

Sample Grant-Writing Course Outline, continued

- Building strong relationships with funders
- Preparing for a funder interview and presentation
- Locating best-fit funding sources
- Disseminating program information

Becoming a Grants Budget Specialist

Study how to build strong, program-oriented grant budgets. Topics include:

- Monitoring grant budgets
- Understanding budget categories
- Creating easy-to-understand budgets
- Writing private and federal budget narratives
- Responding to budget inquiries

The workshop schedule for 2008 is as follows:

Sign Up Deadline	Workshop Date	Topic	Cost	Location
September 5th	March 24–26	Certified Foundation and Corporate Grants Specialist	$400	Millneck, NY
September 20th	April 15th	Developing Strong Budgets	$250	Troy, NY
September 27th	April 25th	Grants Funding Forecast	$300	Princeton, NJ
October 5th	May 3–5	Introduction to Grant Writing	$400	Denver, CO
October 6th	May 7	The Essentials of Grants.gov	$200	Glenwood Springs, CO
October 8th	May 20	Becoming a Certified Grants Specialist	$250	Denver, CO
December 5th	June 5	Becoming a Certified Grants Administrator	$300	Wichita, KS

Freelance Fundraising Consultant

Some grant writers also become qualified to work as freelance fundraising consultants, whom organizations may hire as an alternative to having a full-time professional on staff. Typically, a fundraising consultant might be a professional in a specific field with some experience with fundraising and proposal writing, or a development officer with a small nonprofit service organization in a certain field. The fundraising consultant's job is to look closely at the grant proposal, evaluate how funders may react to it, and make suggestions.

Resource Centers

There are several resource centers where you can further your knowledge about the grant-writing field and become a stronger grant writer.

Associated Grant Makers

Associated Grant Makers (AGM) has a reference collection of publications and other information on foundation and corporate grant making and nonprofit management. The resource center houses national foundations and information about corporate giving as well as IRS 990-PF forms, journals, newsletters, fundraising manuals, and proposal writing guides. AGM is a community of foundation staff and trustees: corporate grant makers, donors, and philanthropic advisory service providers who are working to build a connection with nonprofit leaders. As a warehouse of learning, the AGM provides information for both grant makers and grant seekers that offers grant-related activities every year. Learn more at http://agmconnect.org.

Grantsmanship Center

The Grantsmanship Center is primarily a training organization for grant writers. The center sponsors workshops on writing grant proposals; publishes a funding newsletter, the *Grantsmanship Center Magazine*, which is available free to qualified agencies; and sells reprints of articles related to proposal writing and fundraising. The *Grantsmanship Center Magazine* provides information on how to plan, manage, staff, and get grants for individuals and organizations. Learn more at www.tgci.com.

Working with
Trends in the Industry

At any given time, there are important issues in the grant-industry spotlight. Being aware of topics that are on funders' radar helps you be informed about what fields are in the forefront of philanthropy. For example, during the 1980s, child abuse and early childhood education were high-profile projects. In the mid- to late-1990s, closing the digital divide became a new funding priority, particularly at the federal government level. Other recent trends include professional staff development, cultivating skills in chronically unemployed adults, and gun violence.

Projects That Help Others

A growing trend is the awarding of grants for projects that make a positive difference in the world and offer analytical means of understanding current social and environmental challenges. For example, instead of seeking funding for a research project titled "Rocky Mountain Flowers," which is too general, narrow it down to "Endangered Flowers of the Rockies" or "Therapeutic Flowers of the Rockies." The topic "Therapeutic Flowers of the Rockies" has a specific theme and offers promise of a timely message.

In another example, an arts organization seeking a $20,000 grant to host an exhibit about wildlife preservation has a better chance of winning a grant than an organization seeking funding to travel to Africa on a wildlife safari. Going on a safari is fun, but it offers little promise of helping others or benefiting wildlife.

 Beware!
Grant proposals are not places to be individualistic. You must think of others. It is the grant writer's responsibility to shape the project in a way that offers promise of helping others. The proposed project needs to go beyond the "me" syndrome and move on to "us."

Sticking with Trends

Selecting a project that fits the times is key to a funder's grant-making decision. There are trends in funding priorities among government funders and charitable foundations. For example, since September 11, 2001, projects that address safety and security issues in communities throughout the United States have become especially important. Projects that address anti-terrorism, biological weapons, weapons of mass destruction, and the Middle East have come to the forefront.

Focus Your Idea

The current trend is to fund projects with a sharply defined focus. Funders want to ensure their money is addressing a specific need. For example, let's assume a sculptor is seeking funds to create clay statues about children, to be constructed at a community park. Instead of choosing a broadly defined topic like "children," better shape the idea to convey a specific theme. Introducing the theme of "Children in Unity" and carving images of children holding hands in a circle is a way of giving the sculpture project a sharper focus. Involve the community in producing the project, and the chances of winning the grant are even greater.

Below are some examples showing how you can shape your idea to maximize your funding chances. See the following table illustrates the recommended specific theme.

Grant Proposals on Architecture

Recommended Writing	Grant Topic to Avoid
American Glamour and the Evolution of Modern Architecture	Modern Architecture of the United States
Preserving the Art and Architecture of New Delhi, India	Indian Architecture
The Architecture of Consumption: The Shaping of American Retail Architecture 1960–2000	Retail Stores in the United States
The Art of Lighting in the European Hospitality Industry, 1990–2005	Lighting in Europe
Buddhist Temple Architecture of Asia	Asian Buddhism

Selecting Topics of International Interest

Topics of global concern are hitting closer to home these days. More and more people are traveling and living abroad. Organizations want to help projects overseas and generously award grants help to make that happen.

The tsunami that struck Asia on December 26th, 2004, affected people around the globe. Millions of dollars were given in grants to rehabilitate survivors. An architectural foundation submitted an application, combining the tsunami with architecture. Instead of naming the project "Sri Lankan Architecture," the topic gained a sharper focus when it was re-titled "Post-Tsunami Architecture of Sri Lanka." The example on page 167 is of a project description as it was submitted to a private foundation.

Controversial Topics

Some foundations award grants for projects that make commentaries on topics of social relevance that normally may have difficulty obtaining funding because of their controversial nature.

Projects in this category tend to stir discomforting emotions. They usually are polarized and can be politically disturbing. Whatever your message may be, always remember to communicate it in a way that would make a positive difference in the lives of underserved and oppressed populations.

Beware!
Caution and sensitivity are advised when pursuing controversial topics. There are foundations specifically set up for funding such controversial topics. The Puffin Foundation in New Jersey is one. Visit www.puffin foundation.org.

The issue of working conditions at garment factories in developing countries (also known as "sweatshops") is raising concern among some activist groups. This is a sensitive topic and is usually not discussed at dinner tables. The sample on page 168 is the abstract taken from a project titled "Fashion Fantasy: The Legacy of Garment Factories in Developing Countries."

Genocide and Warfare Topics

Projects that reveal the events in oppressed, war-torn, and remote parts of the world are increasingly receiving the attention of funders. Offering the promise to help a needy community gives your grant proposal an advantage. For example, a

Sample Project Description

Post-Tsunami Architecture of Sri Lanka

"Post-Tsunami Architecture of Sri Lanka" will be a research project to study the architecture and landscape adopted in the southern coast of Sri Lanka since the tsunami ravaged the island's coastlines in December 2004. The purpose of "Post-Tsunami Architecture of Sri Lanka" is to highlight how natural disasters can shape man-made architecture.

Since the tsunami, the southern coast of Sri Lanka has assumed a different kind of architecture and landscape. Hotels are now built on stilts, an architectural framework that is completely new to the Sri Lankan coastal landscape. In residential home gardens, trees and shrubs are carefully picked to withstand the pressures of colossal waves. Instead of growing loose shrubs and tender flower plants that have been traditionally popular in the southern coast, people are now growing a type of seaweed called "Wetaikaiya." This is a shrub that is known for providing a natural barrier for strong waves. During the tsunami some of the hardest hit areas were the ones that did not have the natural buffer provided by the "Wetaikaiya" bushes. The planting of this seaweed on a large scale is beginning to affect the natural landscape of the southern coast.

Before the tsunami, commercial buildings, hotels, and homes were constructed very closely to the beach. After the tsunami, the Sri Lankan government passed a law regulating construction at no less than 100 meters from the ocean. Consequently the pristine beauty of the ocean has become more pronounced. Today, the southern coast can actually be admired in its natural beauty without buildings and houses obstructing its view.

The objectives of the project are to increase our understanding of how the tidal waves shaped the architecture along the southern coast of Sri Lanka and to introduce ocean-resistant architecture for a post-tsunami landscape. The findings will be presented through the form of a video documentary and distributed to environmental organizations, academic institutions, and architectural museums.

photojournalism project on the genocide taking place in Sudan can stir people's emotions, encouraging them to try and make a positive difference, whereas photojournalism proposals on "Temples of Sudan" do not carry the same urgency.

Sample Controversial Topic

Fashion Fantasy:
The Legacy of Garment Factories in Developing Countries

Fashionable garments and apparel are sold in the United States and Europe at higher prices than what it took to manufacture them. While supermodels glorify the glamorous clothing of leading fashion designers, the media generally overlooks the harsh conditions under which these clothes are often produced in developing countries.

The garment industry is the leading export industry in Sri Lanka. Garment factory workers of Sri Lanka are responsible for producing some of the magnificent apparel paraded on the catwalks of Milan, Paris, and New York. They work long hours, and in many cases, are underpaid and overworked to produce this "haute couture" clothing.

"Fashion Fantasy: The Legacy of Garment Factories in Developing Countries" will be a photojournalism project that will recognize the plight of the garment factory workers in developing countries.

Modern Realism

Topics that are peculiar or specific to our times can be classified as modern realism. An example is the alienation caused by modern technology and the corporate world. Cell phones, the internet, and satellites are connecting people technologically while disconnecting them emotionally. Grant requests for programs related to alienation in contemporary society are attracting the interest of funders interested in social science research.

The conflict between tradition vs. modernism is especially poignant in Asian countries such as India, Japan, and Malaysia, where modern trends are seeping slowly into traditional lifestyles. This is apparent in the ancient sacred city of Varanasi, India. A project description to study tradition vs. modernism in Varanasi, India can be found on page 169.

Six Grant-Writing Myths

Myths about grant writing can derail even the most skilled and motivated grant seekers. Don't fall for the traps. Here are some myths to watch out for. Buying into any of these myths can keep success at arm's length for many grant writers.

Sample Modernism Topic

Varanasi India: Tradition vs. Modernism

Varanasi, India, one of the oldest living cities in the world, is more than 2,000 years old. In many ways Varanasi captures the essence of India, filled with contrasts between the old order and the new, ancient civilizations versus modernism, and the sacred versus the secular.

Central to the culture at Varanasi is the Ganges River. Millions of people rely on the river for their spiritual and physical sustenance. The Ganges Holy River is the symbol of India's age-old civilization and religious culture. Varanasi is a holy place for devout Hindus who come to be cremated and buried among temples or "ghats" of the Ganges. The death rituals have been carried out for thousands of years. Each year more than 50,000 bodies are burnt in the Ganges.

Death is a vibrant business in Varanasi. This is where the sacred and commercial facets of death comfortably converge. Ministering the dead is a way of life. Today, funeral rites have become an eerie tourist attraction. A traditional ritual that was once considered sacred has now become a modern, lucrative business.

Life and death are intricately woven into the same cultural fabric at Varanasi. The synchronization of the dead with the living creates overtones of the clash between tradition vs. modernism.

The Soma Health Foundation is interested in conducting a research study titled "Tradition vs. Modernism in Varanasi, India." A group of three psychologists and two sociologists will study traditional activities and contrast them with modern trends taking place in Varanasi. The research project will study how traditional rituals are being both assailed and benefited by modernism and globalization.

Myth 1: If You Craft an Excellent Proposal, It Will Be Funded

Not exactly. Even if a grant writer submits an exceptionally persuasive grant proposal, rejection is always a possibility. The grant proposal is not the only factor that determines whether a proposal is funded. Most established grant writers agree that the success of grant proposals depends on four factors:

1. The quality of the nonprofit organization
2. The innovative nature or critical importance of the proposed project
3. The emerging priorities of a funding source or the level of competition in a particular grant-making cycle
4. The skills of the grant writer in building a compelling case.

No matter how carefully and strategically a proposal is prepared, these other factors affect the outcome.

Myth 2: There Isn't Any Money Available. The Grant-Writing Well Has Dried Up

This is not true. Billions of dollars are waiting to be claimed. Furthermore, those who are entrusted with dispersing this money are just as eager to give it away as organizations and individuals are to receive it. With philanthropists such as Bill Gates, Oprah Winfrey, and Warren Buffett, the grant-writing well is flowing quite strongly.

Myth 3: The Avalilable Money Goes to Big, Prestigious Institutions, Not to Individuals or Small Nonprofits

It is true that more than 90 percent of grants are given to nonprofits and that individual applicants qualify only for a meager sliver of funding. It also is true that enormous amounts of money are given to the same institutions, year after year. However, this does not mean that small institutions and individuals do not qualify for—or receive—grants. Small institutions and people who are "unknown" to the general public are getting hundreds of millions of dollars, too. Knowing where to look for the right grants is key. (See Chapter 4.)

Myth 4: Successful Grant Seeking Requires Connections

Connections can help, but they are not required. Connections may play a role in federal grants, but private foundations are open to applications from anyone who meets the guidelines.

Myth 5: The Contact Information of Funders Is Usually Secret

Far from it! By law, philanthropic organizations and federal funders are required to make their charity-giving public knowledge. The 990-PF reports are the tax returns (see Chapter 4) filed by private foundations, and nonprofits are required to disclose their tax returns. Knowing how to research funders is important.

Myth 6: Earning a Living as a Grant Writer Is Not Financially Profitable

Wrong. Although philanthropy has existed for centuries, the demand for grant writers is just beginning to take off. You can earn a profitable living as a grant writer if you correctly learn the art of grant seeking and you have a healthy mix of clients and funders. Grant writers may earn anywhere from $50,000 to $200,000 a year, or more. The amount depends on the writer's level of expertise, the type of funds sought, how fees are charged (commission or by the hour), etc.

Stat Fact

There are more than 200,000 nonprofits in the United States and only a few thousand skilled grant writers.

Tips to
Remember

This chapter deals with what not to do and what to do—reminders of what has been discussed in the book. Take a minute to review some of the important points to starting your own grant-writing business.

▲

No-Nos for Grant Writers

Some things are best to avoid in the grant-writing business. Being aware of the no-no's can increase your chances of becoming a successful grant writer.

Don't Work for Organizations that May Be Misusing Public Funds

The nonprofit sector has seen increased levels of scandal and fraud. Unfortunately, many shady individuals are setting up nonprofits and misuse public funds, spoiling the reputation of all nonprofits. Because of a few, the nonprofit sector as a whole is coming under scrutiny.

As a grant writer, the first and foremost thing to watch out for is fraud. There are hundreds, or maybe even thousands, of nonprofits that fail to meet the rules and regulations of how public money should be spent. They may be legitimately set up but may engage in unlawful use of funds.

Smart Tip

Tip...

If you know of a nonprofit misusing funds or a con artist running a shady nonprofit, inform the FBI, IRS, or local county government.

Before taking on any clients:

- Determine the length of time the nonprofit has been in existence
- Research the director's credentials
- Meet with board members
- Talk to the people in the community about the nonprofit

Careful of Cons

Watch out for con artists running a nonprofit who may use the $100,000 to treat themselves to a house in Aspen, Colorado, with money that should be going to feed the poor. Here are some red flags to detect fraudulent nonprofit organizations: multiple addresses, changing office locations frequently, no way to check on board members, one-person operations, not releasing tax returns, and the inability to check on how previous funds have been used.

Don't Handwrite Proposals

Handwritten proposals are vintage. Use a computer. You may have the best written proposal, but it may most likely be tossed into the garbage bin if it is handwritten. The computer program Microsoft Word® is simple to learn. If you are not a good typist, learn the art.

Don't Overstate the Need or Problem

It is better to present a need that is limited in scope but can be addressed effectively than to have a problem so large that one project won't be a solution. Instead of trying to save the world, focus on a small, manageable portion of the problem. Give a feeling of local instead of global. Reducing teen pregnancies in one town is more manageable than reducing teen pregnancies throughout the world. There should be a balance between the information presented and the scale of the program.

Don't Assume the Funder Is an Expert on Your Subject

Most grant makers are generalists. They probably know something about topics such as Shakespeare, water pollution, and HIV/AIDS, but you should not assume they are familiar with anemones in underwater marine life. Give an explanation of the field being described so the reviewer can better understand your proposal.

Don't be Romantic in the Cover Letter

Sign the cover letter with a light and positive note such as "I look forward to hearing from you" or "On behalf of the Brettonwood Organization for Women, I thank you for considering our grant request." Remember, this is not a romantic letter. Signing off with intimate phrases such as "With loving wishes" or "Hugs and kisses"—is not recommended. Timing your cover letter to get there on Valentine's Day and pasting pictures of Cupid on the application pages is not going to increase your chance of winning a grant either.

Don't Pest the Funder

A lot of people freeze at the mere thought of presenting their idea to a funder only to be told, "No, we're not interested." One fact of life is that not everyone is interested in what you offer. Don't pester the funder after your proposal has been rejected. It is not going to change the decision.

Beware!

When you put down another applicant, it reflects poorly on you. Stay away from back stabbing and manipulation. They make you look insecure and may weigh against your grant application.

Don't Put Down Other Applicants

Don't assume that you are the only applicant capable of carrying out the project. By putting down other applicants, you are likely to hurt your chances of winning a grant. Acting in isolation does not sit well with today's thinking.

Instead, show how your project can complement and/or enhance existing work. In some cases, it may be wise to show how your project can be groundbreaking.

Don't Linger on One Application

Once you submit an application, move on. Never wait until you hear from one funder before working on other applications. The key is to apply continually. Some funders may take up to a year to notify applicants. Putting all other applications on hold for a whole year is not recommended.

Don't Be in Denial

Having a positive attitude is a healthy thing, but stretching into denial is unhealthy. If you have not heard from a funder in more than a year after the date of application submission, it is safe to assume that your project has been rejected.

Tip...

Smart Tip

Don't put all your eggs in one basket. Create a healthy mix of grant applications. Apply for foundation, government, and corporation grants. Spending six months on only one application is not recommended. Work on several simultaneously. Diversifying is key.

Can't Win Them All

Thinking that you are going to win every grant you apply for can deter you from moving forward. Accept the rejection and move on. This actually brings you a step closer to funding. Living in denial keeps you stagnant, whereas accepting realities and planting new seeds keep you flowing.

Don't Use a Cookie-Cutter Approach

A cookie-cutter (or shotgun) approach is when you submit the same proposal to ten funders, without tailoring each application separately. This is unwise because the guidelines for each foundation are different. You may have to reduce the word count, re-label certain sections, and edit text. It is critical to tailor your proposal for each funder and to format your proposal specifically to the funder's request. For example, the contact name of each funder is different. Adjust the cover letter and address it to different individuals. Any foundation officer will feel a twinge of dismay when the foundation's name is wrong.

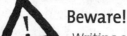

Beware!
Writing a single proposal that can be photocopied and sent to many funders is not recommended. Sending a boilerplate proposal skips the important steps of matching the potential funder with your program, and presenting the match in a way that the funder finds pertinent and compelling.

Speak to each donor's individual interests. Some foundations ask for the "need statement," while others request a "problem statement." Both terms mean the same thing, but titling your proposal accordingly shows that you are tailoring your application to suit the funder.

Don't Work on Commission

No professional wants to work "on spec" and wait for payment when funding comes through. Work on a contract basis—by the hour or on salary. Don't work on commission, unless there is a high probability that you are going to get the grant and the agency has allocated a finder's fee within the grant. For example, if a funder awards a $2 million grant to a public school and your commission is 10 percent, that figure should already be included in the award. Working on commission can be risky business. If a grant is not awarded you will not receive any payment.

Don't Promise a Winning Proposal

Don't ever promise your client that you are going to win a grant within a specific time frame. Seasoned grant writers rarely promise specific results, any more than a lawyer guarantees winning a case. However, as a professional grant writer, you can offer your experience and expertise in good foundation research, analyzing a project, helping your client to structure a well-written grant proposal, writing budgets, and so forth. Although you cannot promise results, if you fail to bring in money over a period of time, most likely your services will be terminated.

Don't Apply If You Don't Qualify

Funders rarely bend their mission statements and make an exception to fund a project that falls outside the guidelines. Funders are not very flexible with their mission statements, unless the funding committee is able to exercise a great deal of discretion for the use of funds. If your project does not fit the grant guidelines, do not pursue that particular source any further. (See Chapter 5.) Save time, energy, and paper, and move to another source.

Don't Submit a Rejected Grant Application without Major Changes

If a foundation has rejected your proposal once and you would like to apply for the following year's cycle, do not simply change the date on the cover page and submit the same proposal. Most likely your application will be rejected a second time.

> **Tip...**
> **Smart Tip**
> Never let rejections end your dreams. Try hard and you will succeed. Yes, you can do it.

Instead, consult the foundation before re-applying. Contact the foundation and find out how you can improve your proposal. Some foundations have a staff officer who provides direct feedback on why the grant application was rejected. These tips can be invaluable in the revision process.

If you can't get a copy of the grant reviewer's comments, ask a veteran grant writer to look at your failed proposal. Rewrite and dress it up before re-submitting.

> **Tip...**
> **Smart Tip**
> Every profession has insider rules for success. They are not posted on any walls and rarely are they written in any handbooks. Rather, they are learned through trial and error. In the trade of grant seeking, adhering to certain rules can increase the chances of getting funded.

Technical Tips for Grant Writers

Simply following the funder's guidelines fills the basic requirements of qualifying for a grant. This helps you get your foot in the door. However, when you are competing with hundreds (and in some cases, thousands) of applicants, merely getting your foot in the door is not sufficient. You have to make your application stand out.

Here are some performance-enhancing technical strategies that can help strengthen your grant application. These are not hard and fast rules, but suggestions that can get you closer to winning grants.

Your First Hello Is Important

Grant seekers often underestimate the importance of the contact letter. In many cases, this letter may be your first and only chance to make a good impression. Reevaluate your logo and letterhead. Most funders prefer organizations that appear professional, not cute. Limit the length of your cover letter to one page or, in some cases, two. Make your presentation as strong as possible and keep it to the point. Check (and double-check) for typographical errors, and ensure that the name of the foundation and your contact are spelled correctly. Above all, submit a clear and readable letter.

Adhere to Deadlines

Develop your own method of keeping track of deadlines. Technologically savvy grant writers can use Outlook. Old-fashioned writers can jot down the deadlines on a calendar or put them on the refrigerator door.

Break Up the Text with Graphs, Charts, and Diagrams

Whenever possible, break up the text. Use reasonable margins, and use bulleted lists and other formatting tools to make each page a little bit more visually inviting. Fifty pages of text can become dry after a while. Introducing pie charts, bulleted lists, spreadsheets, and illustrations (when applicable) is visually soothing for the reader and may get your proposal more attention.

Obtain a Rating Form

A rating form indicates which sections of a grant proposal carries more weight in determining who gets a grant. Most government funders use a rating form to evaluate the quality of grant proposals. As a grant writer, knowing how each section is rated and what kinds of information carry more influence can help you to write more persuasive proposals. Ask the grant agency for a copy of its rating form.

Tip...

Smart Tip

Sometimes reviewers skim proposals, instead of reading every word. Use headings and bullets to make your proposal easy to follow.
Include a table of contents for grant proposals that are more than five pages long. Number the pages.

Pay Attention to Technical Standards and Details

There are technical standards that applicants are expected to follow when applying for grants. Some foundations specify the technical requirements, while others assume applicants are already aware of them. The standard font size for most grant applications is 12. Avoid using fancy font styles; instead use a basic font such as Times New Roman. Keep the typesetting plain instead of bold, unless a title or specific word requires bold writing. Avoid all caps and exclamation points.

Most proposals need to be double-spaced, although occasionally foundations request applicants to submit a single-spaced proposal. Do not justify the proposal (typesetting the manuscript to align perfectly on both sides). Instead, align your proposal to the left.

Define Expected Results

The key to a strong proposal is proving the program's likelihood of achieving its goals. The expected results should be clearly identified and measurement indicators should be outlined. This may not be easy, but the value of having clear performance standards cannot be underestimated. If there are potential problems, it is better to identify and address them before the proposal is submitted.

Edit, Edit, Edit

Edit your proposal several times. The more you edit it, the stronger it becomes. Avoid doing the writing, editing, and submission of the grant application in one sitting. Come up with a fairly finished draft and let it sit for a few days. When you come back, you will notice things you may have overlooked.

Hire a Proofreader

Have someone who is not involved in the project read and critique your draft application. It doesn't need to be someone who is well-versed in the proposed project area, but someone who has a basic command of English. Proofreading is imperative. A separate set of eyes can find typos, poor grammar, and other technical errors that are easy to overlook in your own work. Submitting a proposal with such errors, however, gives the impression that you do not know better or are willing to submit shabby work.

> **Tip...**
>
> **Smart Tip**
> Remember how much better vegetables taste when you allow them to marinate for a couple of hours before grilling? The same principle applies to grant seeking. Allow your draft to marinate for a couple of days. Then, revisit it and edit it.

If you have absorbed all of the information in this book, you are now well on your way to starting a successful grant-writing business. When you believe in yourself and invest the hard work required to make your dreams come true, these positive attributes translate into the day-to-day business of grant seeking.

Appendix A
Grant-Writing Resources

They say you can never be rich enough or thin enough. While these could be argued, we believe you can never have enough resources. Therefore, we present for your consideration a wealth of sources for you to check into, check out, and harness for your own personal information blitz.

These sources are tidbits, ideas to get you started on your research. They are by no means the only sources out there, and they should not be taken as the Ultimate Answer. We have done our research, but businesses do tend to move, change, fold, and expand. As we have repeatedly stressed, do your homework. Get out and start investigating.

Associations

Asian Cultural Council
437 Madison Avenue, 37th Floor
New York, NY 10022-7001
Phone: (212) 812-4300
Fax: (212) 812-4299
www.asianculturalcouncil.org
E-mail: acc@accny.org

The Asian Cultural Council is a foundation supporting cultural exchange in the visual and performing arts between the United States and Asia.

Fellowships to individuals constitute the central feature of the ACC's grant program, the emphasis being on awards to artists, scholars, and specialists from Asia for research, study, and creative work in the United States. Some grants are also made to Americans pursuing similar activities in Asia and to educational and cultural institutions engaged in projects of special significance to Asian-American exchange.

In addition, the Asian Cultural Council awards a small number of grants in support of regional exchange activities within Asia.

Ashoka Foundation
1700 North Moore Street, Suite 2000 (20th Floor)
Arlington, VA 22209
Phone: (703) 527-8300
Fax: (703) 527-8383
www.ashoka.org
E-mail: info@ashoka.org

Ashoka's job is to make "everyone a changemaker." To help create a world where everyone has the freedom, confidence, and skills to turn challenges into solutions. This allows each person the fullest, richest life.

Rather than leaving societal needs for the government or business sectors to address, social entrepreneurs are creating innovative solutions, delivering extraordinary results, and improving the lives of millions of people.

It is this insight into the power of social entrepreneurs that led Bill Drayton to found Ashoka in 1980 and that continues to guide Ashoka today.

Beginning with the first Ashoka Fellows elected in India in 1981, Ashoka has grown to an association of over 1,800 Fellows in over 60 countries on the world's five main continents. Ashoka Fellows work in over 60 countries around the globe in every area of human need.

Global Fund for Women
1375 Sutter Street, Suite 400
San Francisco, CA 94109
Phone: (415) 202-7640
Fax: (415) 202-8604
www.globalfundforwomen.org
E-mail: asiapac@globalfundforwomen.org

The Global Fund for Women supports women's groups that advance the human rights of women and girls. They strengthen women's right groups based outside the United States by providing small, flexible, and timely grants ranging from $500 to $20,000 for operating and program expenses.

The Global Fund supports

- Groups of women working together.
- Organizations that demonstrate a clear commitment to women's equality and women's human rights.
- Organizations that are governed and directed by women.
- Organizations based outside of the United States.

The Global Fund does not support

- Individuals and scholarships
- Organizations that do not have a women's human rights focus.
- Organizations headed or managed by men.
- Organizations whose sole activities are income-generation and/or charity.
- Organizations based or working primarily in the United States.
- Organizations in the Global North proposing partnerships in the Global South.
- Government entities, political parties or election campaigns.

The Grant Advisor
248 Marilyn Circle
Cary, NC 27513
Phone: (919) 461 1649
Fax: (919) 882 9465
E-mail: info@grantadvisor.com

Since 1983, The Grant Advisor newsletter has been a leading source of information on grant, research, and fellowship opportunities for U.S. institutions of higher education and their faculties.

The Grant Advisor newsletter comes in two versions: (1) the PAPER VERSION is a great value at only $237 for a one year subscription, mailed each month (except July); (2) the WEB VERSION, $467/year (The Grant Advisor *Plus*) offers on-line access for your entire institution and features many extras, including the newsletter in Acrobat PDF format, database searches, deadline listings with extensive hyperlinks, and much more, all in an easy-to-use web interface.

Grantsalert
P.O. Box 38051
Tallahassee, FL 32315-8051
Phone: (850) 385 0488
Fax: (850) 385 8546
www.grantsalert.com

Grantsalert is a center that teaches how to write grant proposals, how to find grant writers, latest updates in the world of philanthropy, and all other details pertaining to grant seeking and grant giving. It is an excellent free source for beginner level grant writers and those interested in starting their own grant writing business.

LRP Publications
747 Dresher Road, Suite 500
P.O. Box 980, Horsham, PA 19044
Phone: 800 341 7874
Fax: 215 784 0860
www.lrp.com

Founded in 1977 by Kenneth Kahn, a practicing employment law attorney, LRP (then known as Labor Relations Press) first published case reporters for the legal profession. As the company grew, it became known as LRP Publications. For 25 years, LRP's fast-paced, results-oriented environment has helped it to expand – both internally and externally. LRP publishes both *Human Resource Executive* magazine and *Risk and Insurance* magazine and more than 120 newsletters in the fields of human resources, workers compensation, education administration, law, and higher education. Major web sites include Educationdaily.com, Workindex.com, Specialedconnection.com, cyberFeds.com and HREOnline.com.

In addition to its many professional resources, LRP Publications also provides more than 40 top-quality training and educational development seminars, conferences, trade shows, and symposiums.

Government Agencies

Federal Register
www.gpoaccess.gov/fr/index.html

Published by the Office of the Federal Register, National Archives and Records Administration (NARA), the *Federal Register* is the official daily publication for rules, proposed rules, and notices of Federal agencies and organizations, as well as executive orders and other presidential documents.

FirstGov
www.firstgov.gov

The first-ever U.S. government web site that provide easy, one-stop access to all federal government online information and services.

Grants.gov
www.grants.gov

Grants.gov is your source to find and apply for Federal government grants. The U.S. Department of Health and Human Services is the managing partner for Grants.gov.

USA Government Grants
18 W 30th Street
New York, NY 10001
Phone/fax: (201) 221-8190

U.S. Department of Health and Human Services
Office of Grants
200 Independence Avenue, SW
HHH Building
Washington, DC 20201
E-mail: support@grants.gov

Useful Web Sites

Associated Grant Makers
55 Court Street, Suite 520
Boston, MA 02108
Phone: (617) 426 2606
http://agmconnect.org
E mail: agm@agmconnect.org

Associated Grant Makers is a resource center for philanthropy. It has a reference collection of publications and other information on foundation and corporate grant making and nonprofit management including national foundations, corporate giving, IRS 990-PF forms, journals, newsletters, fundraising manuals, and proposal writing guides.

Catalog of Federal Domestic Assistance
www.cfda.gov

The Catalog of Federal Domestic Assistance lists federal grant opportunities. The online *Catalog of Federal Domestic Assistance* gives you access to a database of all federal programs available to state and local governments; federally-recognized Indian tribal governments; Territories (and possessions) of the United States; domestic public, quasi-public, and private profit and nonprofit organizations and institutions; specialized groups; and individuals.

Council on Foundations
1828 l Street NW
Washington DC 20036
Phone: (202) 466 6512

Fax: (202) 785 3926

www.cof.org

Provides links to other sites such as Government Grants Sources and Private Sector Foundations.

The Foundation Center

79 Fifth Avenue, 16th Street

New York, NY 10003-3076

Phone: (800) 424 9836; (212) 620 4230

http://fdncenter.org

Established in 1956 The Foundation Center is dedicated to serving grant seekers, grant makers, researchers, policymakers, the media, and the general public. The Center's mission is to support and improve philanthropy by promoting public understanding of the field and helping grant seekers succeed. Foundation Center Newsletter www.fdncenter.org/newsletters/index.html

Foundation Center Newsletters are free and include *Philanthropy News Digest*, *RFP Bulletin*, *Job Corner Alert*, news from the Foundation Center and news from various libraries.

The Grantsmanship Center (TGCI)

www.tgci.com

The Grantsmanship Center is primarily a training organization. The Center sponsors workshops on writing grant proposals; publishes a funding newsletter, *The Grantsmanship Center* magazine, available free to qualified agencies; and sells reprints of articles related to proposal writing and fundraising. The Center deals primarily with government agencies and nonprofit agencies and concentrates on grant seeking organizations rather than on individual grant seekers.

Guidestar

4801 Courthouse Street, Suite 220

Williamsburg, VA 23188

Phone: (757) 229-4631

www.guidestar.org

E-mail: customerservice@guidestar.org

GuideStar provides information on the programs and finances of American charities and nonprofit organizations, grantmaking activities, up-to-date stories on philanthropy, and a forum for donors and volunteers.

www.fundsnetservices.com

Sources for grants, fundraising, grant writing, and philanthropy online since 1996. Categorized links to other sites.

www.mickeys-place-in-the-sun.com
  The web site home page is divided into three sections: 1) community resources; 2) funding resources; and 3) additional resources. The community resources section lists several categories of funding including education, health, and community development. The funding resources section lists thousands of listings of funders. This web site is free and is user friendly.

Books

Barbato, Joseph, and Danielle S. Furlich. *Writing for a Good Cause: The Complete Guide to Crafting Proposals and Other Persuasive Pieces for Nonprofits.* (New York: Fireside, 2000).

Blum, Laurie. *Complete Guide to Getting a Grant: How to Turn your Ideas Into Dollars.* (Crofton, Maryland: Poseidon Press, 1993).

Brown, Larissa Golden. *De-Mystifying Grant Seeking—What you Really Need to Do to Get Grants.* (New York: Jossey-Bass Publishers, 2001).

Carlson, Mion. *Winning Grants Step by Step.* (New York: Jossey-Bass Publishers, 1995).

Carter, Cheryl. *Grantseeker's Toolkit: A Comprehensive Guide to Finding Funding.* (New York: John Wiley & Sons, 1998).

Edelson, Phyllis, ed. *Foundation Grants for Individuals.* (New York: The Foundation Center, 2003).

Grants Program. *Directory of Grants in the Humanities 2005/2006.* (Phoenix, AZ: Oryx Publishing, 2005).

Klein, Kim. *Fundraising for Social Change.* (New York: Chardon Press, 1996).

Lesko, Matthew, and Mary Ann Martello. *Grants Directory.* (Information, USA, 2002).

Mcllnay, Dennis P. *How Foundations Work: What Grantseekers Need to Know About the Many Faces of Foundations.* (New York: Jossey-Bass Publishers, 1998).

New, Cheryl Carterm, and James Aaron Quick. *How to Write a Grant Proposal.* (New York: John Wiley & Sons, Inc., 2003).

Orosz, Joel J. *The Insider's Guide to Grantmaking.* (New York: Jossey-Bass Publications, 2000).

Paulson, Ed, and Marcia Layton. *The Complete Idiot's Guide to Starting Your Own Business.* (New York: Alpha Books, 1998).

Reif-Lehrer, Liane. *Grant Application Writer's Handbook*. (Sudbury, MA: Jones and Bartless Publishers International, 2005).

Savage, Jack. *The Everything Home-Based Business Book*. (Cincinnati, OH: Adams Media Corporation, 2000).

Smith, Nancy Burke, and Judy Tremore. *The Everything Grant Writing Book*. (Cincinnati, OH: Adams Media Corporation, 2003).

Wason, Sara D. *Webster's New World: Grant Writing Handbook*. (New York: Wiley Publishing, 2004)

White, Virginia. *Grant Proposals that Succeeded*. (New York: Plenum Press, 1983).

Appendix B
A Brief History of Philanthropy

The United States has a long and rich history of philanthropy and giving. The long-standing tradition of caring for others and sharing blessings dates back to American Indians who shared their harvests and knowledge with the new European settlers.

Since the country's beginning, when one family had a need, others pitched in to help—knowing that if they were ever in the same position, the community would respond in a like fashion. These are the humble roots of American philanthropy.

▲

In the course of centuries, the federal government's role in philanthropy exploded. With passage of the federal Tax Act in 1913, the federal government established an income tax program through which it collected money, then redistributed it wherever it was most needed throughout the United States. Today, the American government predetermines the types of projects and programs that need public support and then, through its various federal agencies, identifies exactly where the funding should go through requests for proposals, or RFPs (see Chapter 3 for more information about RFPs).

Individual, family, and community philanthropy, which preceded government philanthropy preceded federal government funding. Ben Franklin was one of the earliest philanthropists, both with his money and time. He gave to causes that worked to provide equal opportunities for community members as well as volunteered at his local hospital, library, and fire department.

Andrew Carnegie was among the first of the turn-of-the-century industrialists to promote "giving back." Carnegie was joined by such notables as John D. Rockefeller and Margaret Olivia Sage, wife of wealthy industrialist Russell Sage, who channeled his bequest to her into programs that strengthened education and encouraged social reform. These early millionaires established formal philanthropic foundations modeled after their successful business practices. The Federal Act of 1969 was a key factor in promoting philanthropic activities among individuals and businesses.

The passage of the 1935 Revenue Act allowed corporations to deduct charitable contributions from their federal income taxes, providing an incentive for corporate giving and eventually leading to more accurate reporting of philanthropic activities. World War II brought a dramatic rise in philanthropy as well as an increasing need for support for social welfare causes in the United States and abroad.

Corporate philanthropy began in the late 19th century when railroad companies supported the YMCA, ultimately helping to provide safe housing for railroad workers. By the early 1960s, nearly half the states in the United States had legally authorized corporate philanthropy. By this time, most U.S. companies had established their own in-house foundations. The federal government continued to encourage corporate gifts through deduction provision in the tax laws.

The economic boom of the 1990s created new wealth. A new breed of donors emerged, mostly in the high-tech industry. Today, financial tycoons such as Bill and Melinda Gates and Warren Buffett donate billions of dollars for domestic and international causes.

Glossary

Block grant: Federal grants made under very broad, general subject areas.

Boilerplate: Sections of any document, especially a proposal, that have been used and reused so often that they have become standard elements.

Budget: The financial plan for your grant, itemized to show breakdown of both income and expenses. Graphical representation can be helpful in presenting this information clearly.

Community foundation: A public charity supported by funds contributed by individuals, foundations, nonprofit institutions, and corporations. Giving is located within specific locations (city, county, or state). Donors may designate specific charitable agencies or provide that grants be made for charitable purposes at the discretion of the foundation's public board.

Cost sharing: A method of matching money in which the grantee agrees to invest a certain sum or percentage of "in-kind" dollars into the project.

Direct costs: The total dollar amount necessary to fund the project. This includes cash money only, not indirect costs.

▲

Discretionary funds: Grants that are allocated according to a funder's judgment rather than according to a pre-established guideline or set of criteria.

Endowment: Money contributed to provide a continuing income for support or maintenance. The enowment may be general or specified for a particular project.

Foundation: A foundation is in essence: an endowment—a donor's contribution—which is invested so as to realize an income from which grants are made, and a board or committee that reviews proposals and decides where the money will be placed. There are two general categories of foundation: private foundations (general purpose, special purpose, family, and operating) and public foundations (synonymous with community foundations).

Grantsmanship: The art of knowing where money is and how to get it.

Indirect costs: The overhead an organization has to pay in order to support a grant (electricity, rent for space, parking, etc.).

In-kind: A contribution of services or items that an organization donates instead of a monetary sum (e.g., contributing a staff member's time).

Letter of inquiry: A letter that the grant seeker sends before writing or submitting a grant proposal in order to ensure the proposal fits within the foundation's guidelines and mission.

Letter of support: A simple letter attached as an addendum to your proposal. This letter should be from an "expert" or supporter of your project explaining why he or she believes that your project should be funded.

Matching funds: A dollar amount that the grantee or other outside party agrees to contribute to the project.

Narrative: The written portion of your grant proposal. The story of who, what, where, when, why, and how. Every grant has at least two parts: a narrative and a budget. Often grant guidelines specify that your narrative may not exceed a certain page length. Always adhere to these instructions.

Need statement: The part of the grant proposal in which you explain, using both qualitative and quantitative data, why you should be funded. Remember to outline your problems and give data to verify the problem areas (also called "problem statement").

Objective: Specific, measurable aims for project, with matching outcomes to measure them.

Project director: The individual responsible for activities involved in the grant, including the evaluation and follow-up (also called "coordinator").

Request for proposal (RFP): A notice from a funding agency or foundation to solicit proposals for new grant opportunities. RFPs usually list program descriptions, deadlines, and eligibility requirements. Grantseekers should send a letter of intent and request an application packet.

Target population: The intended beneficiaries of a grant-supported service project (also known as "client population").

Tax exempt: A legal status, bestowed by the Internal Revenue Service, which states that organizations have adequately demonstrated their charitable, educational, religious, scientific, or literary nature. By far the largest part, but not all, of tax-exempt organizations are nonprofit corporations. Others include trusts and benevolent associations.

Index